Comedia/Minority Press Group Se~~~ ~~ ~~~ ~

NUKESPEAK
The media and the bomb

Edited by Crispin Aubrey

Comedia Publishing Group
9 Poland Street, London W1V 3DG Tel: 01-437 8954

Comedia Publishing Group (formerly Minority Press Group) was set up to investigate and monitor the radical and alternative media in Britain and abroad today. The aim of the project is to provide basic information, investigate problem areas, and to share the experiences of those working within the radical media and to encourage debate about its future development. For a list of other titles in the Minority Press Group Series, see page 134.

First published in 1982 by Comedia Publishing Group
9 Poland Street, London W1V 3DG. Tel: 01-437 8954

© Comedia Publishing Group and the authors

ISBN 0 906890 26 8 (paperback)
ISBN 0 906890 27 6 (hardback)

Designed by Pat Kahn

Typeset by Manchester Free Press
Bombay House, 59 Whitworth Street, Manchester M1 3WT (061-228 0976)

Printed in Great Britain by
Unwin Brothers Limited, The Gresham Press, Old Woking, Surrey

Trade distribution by

Southern Distribution, Albion Yard, Bldg K, 17A Balfe Street, London N1 (01-837 1460)

Scottish and Northern Distribution, 4th Floor, 18 Granby Row, Manchester M13 (061-228 3903)

Scottish and Northern Distribution, 48a Hamilton Place, Edinburgh EH1 5AX (031-225 4950)

Contents

P
96
O 242
G76
1982

Preface

John Pilger

The great American muck-raking journalist, I.F. Stone, wrote: 'Every government is run by liars, and nothing they say should be believed'. He exaggerated, though not much; governments are the prime source of propaganda, of which lying by degree is the essence. When the First World War was over, Phillip Gibbs, the British correspondent, reflected: 'Some of us wrote the truth from the first to the last, apart from the naked realism of horrors and losses and criticism of facts, *which did not come within the liberty of our pen*'. The italics are mine; the rare honesty is his. In the 1980s with nuclear war a real prospect, the spreading of 'our propaganda' by journalists is no less common than it was during Gibbs' time, perhaps more so. The difference is that then there was a public agonising by journalists; today there is silence.

Since the Second World War, which was generally reported as *simply* a great crusade, as our good guys against their bad guys, war has not fallen into disgrace as some would wish to believe, and certainly not in the media: witness the born-again front page jingo-ism during the Falklands episode. Since Hiroshima 'our side' has promoted a cold war based on a nuclear arms race which has been largely of its own making, and during the period of this arms race we journalists in the Western media have operated a double standard incompatible with a truly free press. Whilst we have rightly dis-missed most of the Soviet Union's posturing as propaganda, we have accepted by and large the lies of our own governments as the truth, and by default or cover-up, and by constantly and insidiously painting 'our side' as the good guys, we have lulled readers and viewers and listeners into a passiveness which has only just begun to change; and, therefore, we have played our part in beckoning nuclear war.

There are subtleties in this conditioning. Since President Truman's announcement of the Hiroshima bombing ('The experi-ment has been an overwhelming success') was uncritically reported, most journalists, in reporting the nuclear arms race, have followed what I would call an 'acceptable bias'. This bias or 'consensus viewpoint' is very often the main ingredient of what governments and officialdom in general like to call objectivity. It is the same 'objectivity' to which broadcasting organisations, in particular, aspire, and it is the same bogus objectivity inflicted on to young journalists, who are taught to confuse scepticism about authority and its propaganda with cynicism about people. In this way the old journalists' fable is handed on: the public 'doesn't care' and, anyway, 'there is no choice'.

From the beginning of the nuclear era, it has been the *duty* of journalists to reject outright jargon which has corrupted the language and conditioned its users, but we have not. We embraced 'Little Boy' and 'Fat Man' and 'hardware' and 'modernised systems' *ad nauseum*. By using reassuring, almost soothing terms, such as 'deterrence', which allowed both the politicians and people to distance themselves from the horror of nuclear war, we actually created new and acceptable images of war and the illusion that we could live securely with nuclear weapons. Did we journalists bother that from 1965 to 1980 the British parliament did not once debate nuclear weapons? Did we rumble a Labour Government secretly and deceptively committed to a vast new nuclear arsenal? With honourable exceptions, the answer is no.

The venerable 'Missile Gap' is my favourite example of the promotion of propaganda in the guise of news. The Missile Gap dominated headlines in the late Fifties and early Sixties. An hysteria swept over the American military when the Russians put Sputnik, the first satellite, into space. This, it was trumpeted, was 'proof' that the Russians were ahead in missile technology. But this was a lie. Indeed, the very notion of a Missile Gap was ridiculous, as virtually every American scientist, working on missiles, now concedes. Dr. Herbert York, in his 1969 book *Race to Oblivion*, described 'a power struggle over who would get the juiciest and sexiest roles and missions in long range missiles. When Sputnik went up each of the services hoped to take advantage of the public confusion and consternation over Sputnik'. And when Dr. York wrote about 'the generating of self-serving intelligence: something which can be found again and again in other debates about nuclear weapons', he might have been describing the Reagan administration's monomania about a Soviet Threat.

Not long ago I went to the Ministry of Defence and received the usual supine 'non attributable' briefing about The Threat. 'What', I asked a public relations man, 'is the Ministry's attitude toward the media? Do you feel you get a good or a bad Press?' Without hesitation, he replied, 'Oh, we get an *excellent* Press.'

As the survival movements gather strength in Europe and the United States, I believe more journalists will join in. The Ministry man did say there were 'worrying exceptions' to his 'excellent Press'. I hope this valuable book is read by journalists, so that the worrying exceptions might become the rule, and people are informed that they *do* have a choice apart from another and final 'experiment of overwhelming success'.

Countdown to doomsday?

*Crispin Aubrey**

Two and a half years ago, in late 1979, the membership of the British Campaign for Nuclear Disarmament stood at just 3,000. The campaign was still languishing in the shadow of its previous period of mass activity during the 1950's and early 1960's. It was just another pressure group with an obviously humanitarian cause but little popular support.

Last autumn, this same organisation was able to muster 250,000 people on to the streets of London for the biggest demonstration ever seen in this country against nuclear weapons. CND now has over 33,000 national members, probably ten times as many supporters in local groups around Britain, and is just one arm of a massive European anti-nuclear movement focussed in particular on forestalling the installation of new American missiles.

The growth of this popular expression of discontent is such that it can hardly now be ignored by the media. In the wake of the wave of demonstrations across Europe last year, for instance, *Time* magazine – the conservative American weekly – devoted 17 pages of its editorial to the nuclear issue, most of that to analysing the causes of what it called 'Europe's Fear'. Instead of a famous politician or film star on the front cover, *Time* used an artist's painting of a grim-faced young demonstrator against a background of clashing Soviet and United States missiles. It is now scarcely possible to open a serious British publication in any week, watch TV or listen to the radio without finding some reference to nuclear weapons.

How this increased coverage has actually dealt with the issue will be investigated by other contributors to this book. But before looking at the media itself, and the information and comment it has

* *Crispin Aubrey is a freelance journalist and author of* Who's Watching You? *– an account of political surveillance and his own prosecution under the Official Secrets Act.*

presented, it seemed important for readers to have an outline of the events which have both led to the growth of the peace movement and made nuclear war a centrepiece of public debate in the West.

It was no coincidence that CND began to grow from late 1979 onwards. For during that period a series of events took place which raised the temperature of the Cold War to a new level unprecedented in recent years. Since that time, the ferocity of East/West ideological warfare, most recently fuelled by events in Poland, has scarcely abated. And this, as we shall see, has had important consequences for the debate on nuclear weapons.

The crucial turning point was the decision by the Soviet Union, in December 1979, to send troops into Afghanistan, just across its southern border. The first units were said to have crossed the frontier on Christmas Day. But although this 'invasion', as Western commentators described it, was justified by the Russians as requested support from a Communist government in severe difficulties with Islamic dissidents (themselves partly fired by the Iranian revolution), in the West it soon became a symbol of Soviet imperialism around the world.

The crisis in Afghanistan had in fact been building up throughout the previous year, with the families of US nationals being 'evacuated' in the summer alongside reports of the successes of Muslim guerilla fighters. But the 'invasion', the direct involvement of the Soviet military, produced an immediate response in Washington. President Carter forced the immediate suspension of a Senate debate on ratification of the SALT II arms limitation agreement and warned the Russians not to interfere in the oil-important Persian Gulf. This, he said, would be regarded as an assault on 'the vital security interests of the United States' and military force would be used to repel it. American warships were moved into the area, and for a period it appeared that the world really was on the verge of a major international conflict.

Throughout the spring and summer of 1979, as Soviet troops showed no signs of being withdrawn and a lengthy campaign against guerilla outposts continued, the debate centred on the participation of NATO member countries in the Olympic Games, due to take place that summer in Moscow. The United States opted out completely whilst the British government played a drawn-out game of moral pressure on the Olympic Committee to withdraw its team.

But as important as these propaganda manoeuvres on the international chessboard is the fact the Afghanistan provided – and continues to provide – a major justification for the more aggressive demands of military tacticians and the defence lobby. In the United

States it led to the fierce underlining of Richard Nixon's famous statement after the signing of the first SALT treaty in 1972: 'No power on earth is stronger than the United States of America today. None will be stronger than the United States in future. This is the only national defence posture which can be acceptable to the United States.'

Two important changes in personnel leant weight to the re-armament lobby which Afghanistan had supported. In May, 1979 Margaret Thatcher had been elected British Prime Minister with a substantial majority. One of her government's first decisions was to increase the pay of the armed forces, a clear indication of a renewed emphasis on defence spending. And whilst other areas of public spending have been repeatedly cut back, as part of the Conservatives' monetarist economic policy, defence has as far as possible been excluded. The philosophy behind this has been a strong anti-Communist line which has consistently followed the American lead. 'By extending her own armaments effort, the Soviet Union compels others to do likewise,' Thatcher announced in her first Guildhall speech (Nov 12, 1979). 'We must see those who could threaten us as they are and not as we would like them to be.'

More importantly, in November, 1979 Ronald Reagan won a landslide victory in the American presidential election. The new President's economic policies turned out to be almost a carbon copy of Thatcher monetarism, and his attitude to foreign policy and defence spending was considerably more aggressive than anything seen during the Carter years. In his first month of office, he announced that defence spending over the following three years would be increased from a 24% share of the total United States budget to over 32%. But it is in the area of nuclear weapons that Reagan has emerged as the prime mover in a potential new twist to the arms race.

To be fair, the Reagan administration has not in fact developed any startling new *policies* about nuclear war. When Reagan took office, in January, 1981, he did inherit three major areas of decision on weapons *systems*, none of which he initiated. The first was over whether to deploy a new range of ICBMs (Intercontinental Ballistic Missiles), the MX (Missile Experimental) system, which would be capable of hitting Soviet targets from United States soil and whose most novel feature was the plan to site the weapons in a vast 'race track' of linked silos, some of which would be decoys. The second was whether to continue with production of the neutron warhead, whose most novel feature was that it could destroy people without killing buildings. The third was over the stationing in Europe of a new 'generation' of 'long range theatre' nuclear missiles in order to 'modernise' NATO's European forces.

What President Reagan brought to these decisions, however, was a new warmongering stance. From his public statements there quickly developed the feeling, especially in Europe, that Reagan and his advisers wouldn't just push for as much nuclear firepower as they could get, but if pushed themselves, would actually use it. The old swashbuckler from the movies became the new, frighteningly belligerent President with his finger on the button which could annihilate the world. But to understand how Reagan has simply placed a more foreful emphasis on policies already in existence, it's worth looking briefly at how United States – and NATO – defence policy has developed over the last 20 years.

The United States is the senior partner in the North Atlantic Treaty Organisation. It possesses a massive armoury of nuclear weapons on its own territory targeted at the Soviet Union, a large submarine fleet, long-range bombers but also a range of missiles based in Europe, some small enough to be used from tanks. The destructive power of just one of the Americans' largest missiles, the Titan, is equivalent to nine million tons of TNT. (In Europe, Britain and France also have their own independent nuclear armouries, though the French are not necessarily committed to using theirs within NATO). And though the Americans are often viewed by European military strategists as their guardian angels, the US interest is not purely philanthropic: a stable Europe forms an essential part of Western capitalism.

Until the late 1950's and early 1960's, it was assumed that the defence of Europe would ultimately depend on the threatened use of such destructive weapons that neither side would actually use them. This in effect meant the US-based ICBM's, such as the Titan, and the policy is commonly described as MAD, or Mutually Assured Destruction. Given far greater Warsaw Pact conventional capability – that is conventional, non-nuclear manpower and fire-power – the argument ran that only this threat would deter those forces from over-running Europe should a war break out. (NATO planning still assumes that the most likely spark-point for World War III will be the West/East German border.)

It was the American realisation, as Soviet developments in nuclear weapons consistently matched their own, that an all-out nuclear war could be disastrous for its own territory, even if the conflict originated elsewhere, that has led to the concept within NATO of 'flexible response'. Part of this policy is that both weapons, and strategy, have been developed to envisage not just the total destruction of large areas of population but with specific military targets in mind. This change in thinking was given formal status by President Carter's Presidential Directive 59 of July, 1980.

But at the heart of 'flexible response' thinking is the argument that deterrence can only work if the other side believes you can respond effectively to different war situations. Thus a 'ladder of escalation' is created which starts with 'battlefield' nuclear weapons of a few miles range, works up through longer range 'theatre' weapons and ends with 'strategic' intercontinental systems, each rung providing its own deterrent capacity. The other side of the coin, however, is that 'flexible response' has resulted in detailed policies which not only foresee a nuclear exchange in which the superpowers hold back their major arsenals, but that this war could be won. Hence the concept of a 'limited nuclear war' − with the battlefield being Europe.

All this, of course, is based on the premise that the next World War will result from Soviet agression or imperialism. This is the scenario, for instance, of 'The Third World War', a book written by General Sir John Hackett and others in 1978. In this account, a massive Russian invasion of Western Europe is only forestalled by a brief exchange of nuclear weapons which the Soviet Union wisely chooses not to escalate. The casualties, nonetheless, are large areas round the cities of Minsk and Birmingham. But, most importantly, the book is in essence a propaganda exercise for re-arming the West. The war could not have been won (in 1983), it argues, but for the intensive bolstering of NATO's forces. Afghanistan has since provided the impetus for that rearmament.

Of the three areas of decision which faced the incoming US President in early 1981, the most controversial for Europeans was the proposed introduction, starting in 1983, of two new US weapons systems − the Tomahawk ground-launched cruise missile and the Pershing II extended range missile. Both are innovatory. The cruise, a small pilotless aircraft, can travel up to 1,500 miles, hug the ground below radar detection limits and eventually explode with extreme accuracy on its target. The Pershing II, a ballistic missile fired like a rocket, has even greater targeting accuracy but most crucially, could reach Moscow from West Germany in just four minutes. Both, for the first time, would place large areas of the Soviet Union within the range of NATO's land-based European nuclear forces.

Though coincidental, the decision by NATO to deploy the new cruise and Pershing missiles was taken only weeks before the Soviet intervention in Afghanistan. On December 12, 1979, a NATO meeting in Brussels approved the siting of 108 Pershing II and 464 cruise missiles in Europe. The weapons would be under United States control and would be sited in West Germany, Holland, Belgium, Italy and Britain.

As already indicated, the initial development of the cruise (a totally new weapon since the Pershing II is an improved version of the Pershing I, already sited in West Germany) was started many years before the 1979 NATO vote. In January, 1977, the US Director of Defence Research, Malcolm Curie, noted that 'the advent of long range, highly accurate cruise missiles is perhaps the most significant weapon development of the decade...' Official estimates set the development and production costs of cruise missiles (to be borne by the United States) at $5 billion.

Why then has the cruise/Pershing decision aroused so much public concern in Western Europe? Firstly, because the weapons are seen as deliberately provocative to the Soviet Union. This is partly because of their new potential and partly because the official justification for them − that Russia has overtaken NATO in the 'theatre' nuclear arena with its own SS 20 missiles − is viewed as deceptive. In itself, this has created a renewed debate about whether parity in firepower exists between the two opposing blocks

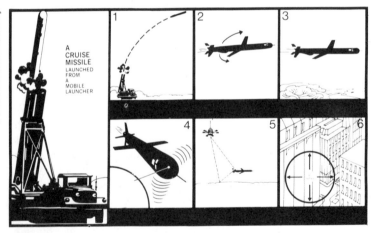

How the cruise missile works, from launch to pinpointed city centre target.
1) It shoots upwards like a rocket but quickly levels out and flies like a plane. 2) The missile is highly manoeuvrable, using wings to change course automatically during flight. 3) It is low flying at about 200 metres flying around physical obstacles close to the ground and avoiding radar and other defences. 4) The missile has a map of Europe and the Western USSR programmed into its computer memory. It can change course to avoid being shot down or detected. 5) Guided by United States global positioning satellites in orbit around the earth, the cruise missile is extremely accurate. 6) It will detonate a nuclear warhead with about ten times the power of the Hiroshima bomb within a radius of 30 metres from any given target.

or, as NATO strategists claim, the USSR is way ahead. Numerous rival statistical analyses have been produced, ranging from the British-based International Institute for Strategic Studies to the Swedish Peace Research Institute, and most recently involving much-publicised official breakdowns by Soviet and US military experts. In the middle, the peace movement's argument that 'if there are enough nuclear weapons now in Europe to destroy the continent 30 times over, what does it matter if one side can do it 14 times and the other 16?' (E.P. Thompson, *Guardian*, Nov 30, 1981) has tended to get lost.

Secondly, the new weapons are viewed correctly as an important development of the 'flexible response' strategy. Their speed and accuracy has even led them to be described as 'first strike' missiles, a claim their originators strongly deny. But their presence in Europe would certainly, it is argued, make the countries in which they are sited even firmer targets for attack than they are already. In the much-quoted words of Rear Admiral Gene La Rocque, a former commander of the US Pacific Fleet and now fervent disarmer: 'We fought World War I in Europe, we fought World War II in Europe, and if you dummies let us we'll fight World War II in Europe.' Europe is seen as never before as the inevitable battlefield of the next international conflict.

President Reagan and his advisers have done little to dispel these fears. During 1981, a series of frighteningly contradictory remarks emerged from the administration over NATO nuclear policy. Reagan himself told a White House press conference in October, 1981: 'I could see where you could have the exchange of tactical weapons against troops in the field without it bringing either one of the major powers to pushing the button.' This apparent acceptance of a limited nuclear war was quickly supported by Secretary of State General Haig, who described a 'nuclear demonstration shot' as a necessary deterrent to Soviet conventional power. But within days Defence Secretary Caspar Weinberger announced that there was nothing in current plans 'that even remotely resembles this'. Reagan eventually returned to the stage to say that he didn't know which view was correct and was waiting for clarification. Though interpreted as a clash between Haig and Weinberger over their relative status in the administration, these exchanges hardly encouraged confidence in United States clarity over nuclear strategy.

Such statements have also in turn encouraged greater disarray among the European NATO allies over cruise missiles than any other recent decision. The Belgian and Dutch governments, both unstable coalitions, have said they will not agree to accept the new

A nuclear chronology: 1979-1982

1979

May *British general election: Conservative government under Margaret Thatcher returned with large majority. Tories pledged to give high priority to defence spending.*

July Families of United States nationals evacuated from Afghanistan following reports of heavy fighting between Communist government forces and Islamic rebels.

October Soviet President Leonid Brezhnev offers to withdraw 20,000 Russian troops and 1,000 tanks from East Germany, also to reduce number of SS20 missiles in Eastern Europe if NATO refrains from strengthening its nuclear forces.

November *British government announces public expenditure cuts in most areas, but increased spending on defence.*

December 12 NATO agrees to 'modernisation' of its 'Long Range Theatre Nuclear Forces'. This means that 572 cruise and Pershing missiles will be sited in five European countries, including Britain, starting in 1983. Belgian and Dutch governments won't commit themselves until outcome of East/West negotiations is clear.

December 26 United States accuses Soviet Union of airlifting troops into Afghanistan to bolster President Amin's regime. Amin deposed, executed and replaced by Babrak Kamal.

December 30 Soviet troops in Afghanistan now said to number 25-30,000. President Carter says 'serious consequences' will ensue.

1980

January 3 United States Senate debate on the ratification of SALT II arms limitation agreement is suspended on request from President Carter. Reason given is the invasion of Afghanistan.

January 4 Afghani President Kamal says Russia acted to defend his country's independence.

January 11 *British ambassador to Afghanistan recalled. Travel restrictions placed on Soviet diplomats in London.*

January 17 *Six Royal Navy ships sent to Mediterranean to assist US Navy.*

January 22 *British government encourages athletes not to attend Olympic Games in Moscow during summer and attempts to get venue changed.*

January 23 President Carter warns that if Russia attempts to seize control of the Persian Gulf this would be regarded as an assault on 'the vital security interests of the United States and therefore military force would be used'. Economic sanctions started against USSR.

January 24 *British defence minister Francis Pym announces that £1,000 million programme for updating Polaris submarines is nearing completion. This 'gives Britain an effective deterrent into the 1980's', he says.*

January 28 US defence budget to increase by 5%.

January 29 Participation by US athletes in Olympic Games cancelled.

Items in italics are events in Britain.

February 26 *Margaret Thatcher instructs her Ministers to take part in exercises to test contingency plans for nuclear war.*

March 10 *British government allocates £13 million for replenishing stockpiles of emergency foods. Some stored in Gloucestershire since 1968 have gone off.*

March 13 *Eton College pupils claim their school fall-out shelter is too small.*

March 17 *Government handbook 'Protect and Survive' published in order to help the official estimate of 30 million British survivors from a nuclear attack to cope with the aftermath.*

April 2 *British government White Paper on defence shows that defence expenditure will rise by 3½% during 1980/81 to £10,785 million.*

April 17 Portugal re-admitted to NATO's nuclear planning group after a five year absence.

April 29 *Pay rises ranging between 14.5 and 20% agreed for British armed forces personnel.*

May 16 *Young Liberals offer jar of vaseline to Margaret Thatcher as part of a 'nuclear survival kit'.*

May 31 *One day Labour Party conference at Wembley agrees to a series of new policies, including 'no nuclear weapons in Britain'.*

June 3 United States nuclear bombers put on alert and a command post aircraft launched in the Pacific after computer error records a Russian missile attack.

June 6 US B-52 bombers carrying nuclear weapons again alerted for take-off through computer warning of Soviet attack. The Pentagon admits that the same computer was responsible.

June 8 *'Protect and Survive' sells its first 20,000 copies.*

June 17 *British Defence Secretary Pym announces that this country's allocation of 160 cruise missiles will be stationed at Greenham Common in Berkshire and Molesworth in Cambridgeshire. First batch will arrive towards the end of 1983.*

June 29 *Businessman plans underground nuclear-proof homes for sale in North Yorkshire.*

July 1 During visit of West German Chancellor Helmut Schmidt to Moscow, the Soviet Union agrees to start negotiations on the limitation of 'theatre nuclear weapons'.

July 15 *British government announces decision to build four nuclear submarines (to replace the Polaris fleet) to be armed with US Trident missiles and British built warheads. Cost will be £5,000 million over 15 years.*

July 23 *Labour Party National Executive gives official support to CND's planned October demonstration.*

August 1 The Soviet Union says it has withdrawn troops from East Germany as promised in October, 1979.

August 8 35th Anniversary of dropping of first atomic bomb on Hiroshima.

September 11 *Liberal Party national assembly defeats motion supporting unilateral disarmament. Leader David Steel's commitment to NATO and new nuclear weapons supported.*

September 19 Belgian government agrees to take 48 new NATO nuclear weapons if US/Soviet talks are unproductive.

October 2 *Labour Party annual conference votes by show of hands for unilateral disarmament and closure of all nuclear bases on British soil.*

October 10 US/Soviet talks on 'theatre nuclear weapons' in Geneva. Abandoned after a month when no agreement reached on which weapons systems should be included.

October 26 100,000 protesters join CND rally in Trafalgar Square.

November 4 Ronald Reagan elected President of the United States in landslide victory. General Alexander Haig, former NATO Commander, to be Secretary of State.

November 5 *Manchester City Council declares the area a 'nuclear-free zone', banning the manufacture or siting of nuclear weapons. Over 60 other local authorities have since followed suit.*

1981

January 5 Reagan inaugurated as US President.

January 18 Reagan administration announces public spending cuts, but defence spending will rise from a 24% to 32% share of the total budget over three years.

March 3 *Ministry of Defence launches its 'Spring Offensive' - a publicity campaign aimed at supporters of CND.*

April 7 *British civil servants' industrial action over wage claim affects defence establishments, including the Faslane nuclear submarine base in Scotland. Government threatens to bring in troops to keep it functioning.*

June 8 Israeli air force incapacitates Iraqi nuclear power reactor at Ibadan in surprise attack. Reason given is that Iraq was preparing to make a nuclear bomb.

June 11 Over 100,000 beds are reported to be constantly available in US hospitals to receive casualties from a nuclear attack on Europe.

June 25 House of Commons Defence Expenditure committee predicts that cost of new Trident missile system will now reach £6,000 million.

July 6 United States government ends 18-year-old nuclear power co-operation agreement with India because of failure to sign the nuclear non-proliferation treaty.

August 9 President Reagan authorises full production of the neutron warhead. The State Department says they will be stockpiled in America with 'no plans at this time' to deploy them elsewhere.

August 27 *Forty women and children march 110 miles from Cardiff to proposed cruise missile base at Greenham Common. Women's Peace Camp established outside main gates with tents and caravans.*

September 14 Major demonstration in West Berlin against visit of US Secretary of State Haig. Violent clashes with police.

September 19 500,000 trade unionists march in Washington against Reagan's cuts and increased arms spending.

'Square Leg' civil defence exercise throughout Britain envisages bombs on over 100 targets, mainly US bases.

October 2 President Reagan gives go-ahead for MX ballistic missile system in 100 silos around the United States.

Don't worry; it's only a neutron bomb

Tim/Socialist Workers Party

October 10 250,000+ people march in Bonn against new NATO nuclear missiles.

October 18 Socialist party under Andreas Papandreou wins Greek general election. Threatens to withdraw from NATO.

October 24 *200,000+ marchers join biggest ever CND rally in London.*

November 6 *Poseidon missile dropped during routine operation at US base in Holy Loch, Scotland. Radiation risk from detonation of the warhead trigger system avoided.*

November 12 First US Trident submarine, the USS Ohio, launched at Connecticut. Every ship is fitted with 24 missiles, each with 8 nuclear warheads of 100 megaton capacity. Large anti-nuclear demonstrations at 147 university campuses around the United States.

November 18 President Reagan proposes his 'zero option' as the basis for nuclear weapons negotiations with the Soviet Union. Praised by some West European leaders, including Thatcher and Schmidt.

November 21 500,000 anti-nuclear marchers assemble in Amsterdam. This represents 1 in 30 of the total population.

November 29 Anti-Pershing/cruise missile petition in West Germany achieves 1½ million signatures.

November 30 US/Soviet nuclear arms talks open in Geneva. US air-force personnel begin training on operation of cruise missiles.

December 3 US intelligence predicts Argentina will produce atom bomb by late 1983.

December 4 *John Silkin, newly appointed Labour spokesman on defence and disarmament, says Britain should abandon nuclear weapons.*

December 6 South Pacific island reported to be 'sinking' into sea after repeated French nuclear tests.

December 13 Martial law introduced in Poland after steadily growing support for Solidarity 'free trade union' and threat of military intervention by Soviet Union. Austrian Chancellor describes the following week as 'the most dangerous since World War II'.

December 19 *Opinion poll records 60% of Scots in favour of removal of all US bases.*

December 29 *Second 'peace camp' established at proposed cruise missile base at Molesworth, Bucks.*

December 30 President Reagan announces sanctions against Soviet Union for its 'heavy and direct' responsibility for Polish martial law. Also threatens to stop Geneva arms talks.

Pentagon official reveals plan to deploy new nerve gas bomb at US bases in Britain.

1982

January 13 *Ministry of Defence revealed to have secretly embarked on replacement of Polaris system's rocket motors. Cost estimated at 'several hundred million pounds'.*

February 3 *Greenham Common peace campers threatened with eviction after work starts on preparing base for cruise missiles.*

February 4 US military budget for 1983 set to rise to 260 billion dollars, 15% up on 1982. Parallel cuts necessary in domestic budget.

President Brezhnev challenges US to reduce number of medium range missiles by 'one third or less' by 1990.

February 14 *British government reported to be considering buying larger, and more expensive, Trident missile system from US.*

February 22 *Seventy-three British MPs join new CND parliamentary group.*

February 23 *Decision by Clwyd County Council means that all eight Welsh counties are nuclear-free zones.*

March 1 American missile stockpiles predicted to grow to total of 40,000 warheads.

March 2 The Soviet Union says it has 'frozen' deployment of SS20 missiles in Europe for three months. Offer to continue freeze if cruise and Pershing 'modernisation' is cancelled later rejected by NATO.

March 4 *British government announces formation of new Home Guard unit to help in 'times of crisis'.*

March 11 *Britain confirms order for more advanced US Trident II missile system, at cost of £7,500 million.*

March 18 'Arms freeze' movement in US reported to be gaining momentum. Gallup poll shows 72% in favour of joint US/Soviet freeze.

March 21 *Mass protest at Greenham Common air base. 39 women arrested for blocking gates.*

missiles until arms limitation talks between the superpowers have run their course. In West Germany, Chancellor Helmut Schmidt has faced considerable pressure from the left wing of his party against NATO policy, and has pegged his political future on acceptance. And all these pressures have been fuelled by the increasingly noisy voices of the European peace movement.

But the 'modernisation' of Europe's nuclear arsenal is not the only decision on nuclear weapons in the past 2½ years to have been stamped with President Reagan's personal seal. Last August, he authorised full-scale production of the neutron warhead, an awesome weapon which operates by releasing enhanced radiation whilst at the same time reducing its blast effect to a minimum. It is considered particularly useful against tanks on a battlefield and has therefore been planned for use in the European 'theatre'. But the development of such a weapon has inevitably caused outrage at its immoral disregard for human life whilst leaving human artefacts unscathed. Reagan has also given the go-ahead for the MX missile system, though how it will be deployed is still at issue, and is reported to be considering a multi-million dollar improvement programme for US chemical weapons, including the basing of nerve gas in Britain.

All these decisions have been given even greater relevance, however, by the attitude of the British government since the election of the Tories in 1979. Margaret Thatcher is not only a firm soul-mate of Reagan, strongly anti-Communist, but has consistently supported all American moves in the nuclear field.

To start with, the British government was the first among the European NATO allies to decide on specific sitings for cruise missiles. Six months after the crucial Brussels vote, Defence Secretary Francis Pym announced that Greenham Common in Berkshire and Molesworth in Cambridgeshire, both RAF bases, would be the twin sites for this country's 160-strong allocation of missiles. Pym himself visited the areas and assured local residents that the missiles will be a comparatively quiet and unobtrusive development. In fact, during a period of 'rising international tension', the missiles would be loaded on to large mobile transporters and dispersed, ready for firing, within a radius of up to 200 miles from their home base. Against a background of increasing concern that this makes much of southern and central England a new potential target, both proposed bases now have CND-supported peace camps outside their main gates. This hasn't, however, stopped initial conversion work from taking place.

Thatcher's defence team has also given Britain's own 'independent' nuclear forces their biggest financial boost in recent years. In July, 1980 it was announced that the four nuclear-armed Polaris submarines — originally introduced in the late 1960's as the main thrust of this country's 'independent deterrent' — would be replaced with the newer Trident version. Each of these new submarines, as long as two football pitches, will be capable of carrying 16 nuclear missiles, and the cost of the project, then £5,000 million, has already been drastically increased. Meanwhile, Polaris itself has been updated, at a cost of £1,500 million, in order to keep it 'competitive' until its replacement is ready in the 1990's. Little public debate, in parliament or elsewhere, accompanied these important commitments.

But even if the argument is accepted that none of these new nuclear weapons makes war more likely, that they're essential to keep the deterrent effective, then there has equally been increased activity in an area which *does* bring nuclear conflict extremely close to home. Emphasised by the publication of 'Protect and Survive' — the easily satirised guide to what the average family can do before, and when, the bomb drops — the government has launched a major campaign to encourage participation by both local authorities and the general public in what is now called Home Defence.

Up to £45 million (1983/4) is now available from central government funds to help local councils and other organisations to employ additional personnel, such as emergency planning officers, build fallout protective bunkers for selected bureaucrats, and draw up emergency plans for maintaining some semblance of order after the holocaust. Around the country, parish councils have been meeting to nominate their own war teams whilst a series of 'war games' has been played out nationally — notably 'Operation Square Leg' in September, 1981 — during which the network of emergency government has attempted to cope with the immediate death of millions of people. Alongside these civil exercises, NATO has carried out some of its own elaborate war scenarios.

There is little doubt that the publicity given to civil defence preparations has in itself encouraged a doomsday atmosphere. Opinion polls show that a record number of people now believe that a nuclear war will occur in their lifetime, a feeling which the Conservative government, despite its public pronouncements, has hardly dispelled. Commenting on the new Home Defence measures, Home Office Minister Leon Brittan said that a policy of military deterrence was only credible if the country was prepared for the effects of war. Military and civil preparedness were closely related, he said (*Times*, Feb 22, 1980). Margaret Thatcher has herself carefully gone through the steps she would have to take to launch a Polaris missile strike. 'Senior officials have never known such close ministerial interest in their "doomsday" activities,' *The Times* reported (Feb 26, 1980).

Reaction outside government to the home defence explosion has ranged from the grimly humorous, such as the classic advice that you should dust radioactive frogs before cooking and eating them, to the realisation that war plans include such oppressive measures as the immediate internment of 'subversives'. Arguing that home defence against a nuclear attack is useless anyway, and simply encourages warmongering, over 100 local authorities, following the lead of Manchester City Council, have either refused to cooperate or declared themselves 'nuclear-free zones'. West Midlands Regional Health Authority has also refused to appoint government-funded staff to plan for 'emergency' hospitals. The private sector has responded to the panic by selling household fall-out shelters for the back garden and by selling plots in mass shelter parks, rather like wartime caravan sites.

One other important series of events has drawn attention to nuclear weapons, and their possible use, over the past two years. For while an increasingly aggressive front has been presented by both Britain and the United States, a continuing propaganda war has been fought between the two superpowers themselves.

The terrain for these exchanges has been the possibility of some *reduction* in the numbers of nuclear weapons, or at least a limitation to the arms race. When President Reagan took office the position was particularly dead on this front: the most recent US/Soviet negotiations – SALT II – had failed to be ratified by the United States, and the record of previous international agreements was hardly impressive. But since the crisis in Afghanistan both sides have made strenuous efforts to persuade the rest of the world that they really do want to stop the arms race.

The opening salvo was fired by the Soviet Union. In October, 1979 President Brezhnev offered to reduce the number of SS20 missiles targeted at Europe if NATO agreed to abandon its 'modernisation' programme. The offer also included the withdrawal of 20,000 troops and 1,000 tanks from East Germany, a move said to have been completed a year later. President Carter in turn described the Soviet offer as 'an effort to disarm the willingness or eagerness of our allies adequately to defend themselves.' But during the autumn of 1980, following a visit by Chancellor Schmidt to Moscow, negotiations between United States and Russian representatives on 'theatre nuclear weapons' *did* begin in Geneva, though they failed to make much progress.

In the wake of the controversy over the cruise/Pershing decision, Brezhnev repeated his offer, though its treatment in much of the Western media was as an attempt to capitalise on the growing peace movement, a movement which the Russians were said to have directly financed to the tune of many millions of dollars. Nonetheless, feeling left out of the international diplomatic stakes, and pressured by European discontent, President Reagan eventually proposed last November his oddly titled 'zero option'.

The 'zero option' is in essence a deal in which NATO doesn't proceed with its theatre weapons 'modernisation' only if the Soviet Union dismantles all its SS20s (some of which are sited on the Chinese border) as well as its older SS4 and SS5 missiles. Eagerly applauded by both British and Western German politicians, the deal has been criticised as totally unacceptable to the Russians (who argue anyway that a crude balance in nuclear forces already exists) and labelled a 'propaganda stunt'. But after immediately dismissive comments from the Soviet leadership, talks between the two sides opened again in Geneva soon after Reagan's zero option announcement. At the time of writing, they are still in session. Given the subsequent introduction of martial law in Poland, and the US accusation of Soviet manipulation, their chances of meaningful progress seem slim.

Throughout this period since Afghanistan, there has obviously also been a steady chorus of demands from the European peace movement for an end to the superpowers' 'race towards Armageddon' (see chronology for important events), and its influence has clearly been felt in the corridors of power both of Europe and across the Atlantic. One interpretation of the 'zero option' was that Reagan would not have made his offer − against the advice of some of his military tacticians − but for the existence of that pressure. But it's also true that alongside the ability of the US government to, for instance, transmit satellite pictures of Reagan's speech to over 2 million TV viewers around the world, the resources of the peace movement are minimal. The British Ministry of Defence has an army of press officers, ready not only to produce propaganda in defence of 'deterrence' but to maintain a steady supply of 'human interest' stories of military life to the local and national press. CND has just appointed its first and only press officer. How the media has responded to those conflcting, and unequal, demands on its attention is the subject of the remainder of this book.

Part 2   Deadlines: the war of the words

Peace in our Times?

*Ian Connell**

'Now, what's very interesting with the peace movement today is we've used, if you like, pre-modern means of communication, bringing a movement from the bottom up – from the platform, the pamphlet, the pulpit, the small public meeting – without the help of television and the mass media at the beginning. You see we're operating against a whole well-funded establishment which is determined to present our ideas as if eccentric or queer.'

—E.P. Thompson in 'The Disarmament Man'
(World in Action, *Oct 20, 1981*)

Edward Thompson's remarks demonstrate a quite considerable confidence in the capacities of what he calls the 'pre-modern means of communication'. With them, and them alone, so it would appear, a popular movement now numbering in the region of a quarter of a million (the most recent estimate of CND's membership alone) has been built. The building of this movement has not only been without assistance from the media – from television, radio and the press. It is also Thompson's suggestion that the movement has been put together in spite of and against what these media have been doing; for they *are* the presentational vehicle for that 'well-funded establishment'.[1]

This view is not Thompson's alone. It has been taken up and developed by, for example, Mediawatch – an organisation set up to 'increase awareness about the misrepresentation and neglect of the peace movement by the media'.[2] Over the last year there have been several TV programmes devoted to the issues raised as both American and NATO nuclear arsenals are considered for 'modernisation'. Noting a number of these, Gari Donn, of Glasgow University, concludes that all this coverage has resulted only in 'disinfor-

* Ian Connell is a senior lecturer in communications studies at Coventry Polytechnic. He has researched and written extensively about the media, especially current affairs and documentary television.

mation'. The media, she says, stereotype disarmament positions:

... debates about the nature of the Cold War, the rising heat in the international situation and the possibility of grass roots, mass movement led action are non-issues, they are not 'newsworthy'. Therefore, in the sense that the media create political possibilities for action, we can see a whole spectrum of possible anti-nuclear action being 'written out', made nonsense of, and more worryingly, made part of the extremist, lunatic (now Soviet funded) CND fringe.[3]

What is more, such a media-generated stereotype becomes, she asserts, 'the "common sense" view of what the nuclear debate is about'. In other words, most people 'understand' the issues, and the nature of the opposition to nuclear weaponry and its deployment in Europe, specifically in those terms which are employed by television, radio and the press to tell their nuclear stories.

It would be fair to say, I think, that these are reasonably typical peace movement views. There are others, not fundamentally at odds with those outlined here, which would stress more emphatically the existence of a Ministry of Defence led conspiracy to counter and 'rubbish' CND. In this conspiracy, journalists and broadcasters are pictured as either willingly (particularly if they work for *The Daily Telegraph*), or unconsciously, colluding. In either case it is assumed that CND doesn't get a fair hearing.

Yet, if they are party to such a campaign to discredit CND and undermine its growing support, some sections of the media would seem not to have acted with an unswerving devotion to duty. According to John Nott, Secretary of Defence, 'the way in which the BBC, in particular, gave prominence by selective quotation to Reagan and Haig's remarks disturbs me. Such selective reporting does not lead to any greater understanding of the security problems of the West. It merely fans the fear of war' (quoted in *The Times* and *The Daily Telegraph*, Nov. 6, 1981). You will probably remember the remarks to which the Defence Secretary was referring: Reagan's was the somewhat jumbled re-affirmation that a nuclear war in Europe (sometimes referred to as a 'limited' nuclear war), not involving the U.S., could be envisaged. Haig's concerned the 'firing of a nuclear weapon for demonstrative purposes'. Both were quite extensively covered by the journalistic media in this country and in Europe. Indeed, some reports commented that the remarks had passed virtually unnoticed by American journalists. Towards the end of November, 1981 *Panorama* previewed the then imminent talks between Haig and Gromyko, in the course of which Haig was interviewed. He too adopted Nott's theme — that the approach of European journalists was such as to stir up concern and to misrepresent the intentions of the Reagan administration.

So it would seem that each party imagines the BBC, if not others, to be agin them – to be 'biased' in favour of the other side. But which is it? Do the media exhibit a clear and unequivocal bias to one side or the other? Do they explicitly advocate either the 'pro-' or 'anti-' nuclear case?

Questions such as these imply that the media can *only* be explicitly for or against, and that their business is one of partisan advocacy. There can be no other option. Needless to say, many people who work in the press and broadcasting would not agree with this. They would argue that they adopt a 'neutral' position, neither 'pro' nor 'anti', that they merely report what has been said and/or done, on that basis speculate as to possible outcomes – and leave the advocacy to those directly involved. Those charging 'bias' usually regard such statements as empty rhetoric or as a worthy expression of intent which is rarely fulfilled in practice.

Again we must ask which is it – partisan advocate or neutral reporter? And while we're asking these questions there are one or two others that ought to be put. Is Edward Thompson right to suggest that the campaign which has been growing throughout Europe has been generated and sustained *without* the assistance of the media? If he is, why then is he and are others so concerned about what the media have to say about the issues of nuclear arms? Have those campaigning for peace not done as Thompson suggests, namely developed the movement in spite of the media? Or, if as Gari Donn has suggested, these media possess an ominous definitional power and by exercising it fashion *common* sense, by what means has she, Edward Thompson and indeed many thousands of others actively campaigning against the possession and deployment of nuclear weapons been able to resist and refuse that power? By those pre-modern means spoken of by Thompson? If so, then does it really matter what the media's stories are, since these other means seem to have served as an effective alternative?

Questions such as these are by no means idle. I would suggest that they are of crucial tactical significance. Why waste scarce resources on attracting the attentions of the media, of professional journalists say, if you have developed an effective alternative?

In my view, no such effective alternative exists. Without wanting to deny the importance of the pamphlet, pulpit and small public meeting, they are, no longer, a substitute for the 'national' and 'international' coverage of which the press and broadcasting are capable. It is also my view that Thompson is wrong to suggest that the movement has been built without any assistance from these professional media of communication. Considerable efforts were

*A rare initiative
from the popular dailies:
seven pages of the* Daily Mirror *(Nov 6, 1980)*

made in the autumn of 1980 and again in 1981 to attract their
attention. I want to suggest that, especially in respect of the 1981
demonstration, the winning of their attentions, while not in every
instance favourable, was not overall entirely disadvantageous to the
organised peace movements.

   Of course it can be argued that had it not been for the considerable efforts of the organisers there would have been no coverage at
all. They, in a sense, initiated the coverage. But this is not always
the case. In 1976, well before the beginning of the CND revival,

Panorama initiated a substantial journalistic investigation of cruise missiles and called it 'The Doomsday Doodlebug'. Among other things Tom Mangold investigated what the cruise missile is, what it is capable of, and whether it would threaten the SALT II negotiations then under way. The programme included interview sequences with the makers of the missile in which they were unable or unwilling to state whether once launched it could be called back – the 'uncertainty' which led Mangold to dub it 'a doomsday weapon'. This programme was an important contribution to growing concern and opposition to cruise missiles.

Lawrence Freedman has suggested that, as decisions concerning the future of Britain's nuclear arsenal could no longer be delayed, defence once again became a major issue on the mainstream political agenda.[4] And, as it became so, programmes like *Panorama* began to speculate about possible consequences. In 1979, the Conservatives were returned to office. They were committed to (and widely reported as being so) continuing with the nuclear programme as a way of countering what Margaret Thatcher had for some time been speaking of as 'the growing dangers of Soviet expansion' and 'the military peril in which the West now stands'.[5] Since that election, press and broadcast journalists have made available much of the information about this government's defence policies, information upon which campaigning has depended. And not only information. The stories they have told have contributed to the fear and suspicion which has led many to active campaigning – upon which the media have subsequently commented, thus amplifying and reinforcing that campaigning.

If this is the case then there is something fundamentally wrong with the conception of the media as 'biased' and with any strategy based upon it. To accuse the media of deliberate misrepresentation ('bias') or to suggest that their authoritative and powerful establishment sources have misled them is not at all productive. This is not to deny that there are instances, some of which will be commented upon in a moment, where stories seem to have been deliberately constructed to discredit CND. However, to note these instances alone would be to note only one aspect. Moreover, the view of the media which only notes these examples is not able to see that while the media may not actively campaign for the organised peace movement, it does not necessarily follow that they actively oppose them.

Indeed it is possible to make out and substantiate a case for seeing the media as not involved in campaigning most of the time. Journalism is mostly involved in reporting, and as this is professionally conducted, it does not make recommendations. Reporting is not neutral therefore, but then neither is it deliberately committed this way or that. The problem is rather that reporting prefers, by quite *undeliberate* means, certain explanations over others. Some seem to make 'more sense' or some may seem more dramatic. But whatever these means are, it is clear that a conception concerned only with *deliberate intentions* is unlikely to identify them or ways of dealing with them.

Yet even this still sounds too negative. Much of the passing criticism so far made of the media tends to presume it has a certain, specific kind of effect. While John Nott and his colleagues no doubt presume a subversive effect, Edward Thompson and his presume one which legitimates the pro-nuclear case. The situation, in my view, is more complex, more open to re-definition than is allowed by this sort of presumption. It might seem that to give airtime to American generals or spokespeople for NATO or the MOD would be to incline the reporting in a very particular direction. But what is the effect of, for instance, Brigadier-General Fulwyler's almost throwaway remark that 'nuclear weapons serve a useful purpose on the battlefield'? When later asked about casualties and whether in a nuclear/chemical conflict it was possible to avoid self-inflicted casualties, he replied: 'All I can say is we would expect significant casualties... entire units might disappear in a flash of an eye' (*The Defence of the United States*, BBC 1, Oct. 1, 1981). Are such unquestioned statements likely to secure support for a nuclear 'deterrent' or not? And what is the effect of being told by David Dimbleby at the outset of the same programme that 'the American army is being taught how to fight a nuclear war against Russia without America being attacked — a war with Europe as the only battleground'? Or of being told by Peter Jessel on *Newsweek* (BBC 2, Feb. 20, 1981) that 'for the Americans, Britain is, in one sense, a giant unsinkable aircraft carrier for planes such as the F111... a launching pad for cruise missiles'? Or what is the effect of being told (in *Panorama*'s 'Re-Arming of America', BBC 1, May 18, 1981, and again in *In Evidence*, 'The Bomb', YTV, Nov. 4, 1981 and in several newspaper articles) that the policy of Mutually Assured Destruction bit the dust with Carter's Presidential Directive 59, which inaugurated the policy of preparing for 'a prolonged but limited nuclear war' based on the assumption (questioned in the programmes referred to) that there can be such a thing as 'a fight-able and winable nuclear war'? Are these really the themes that will secure public consent for a modernised, independent nuclear deterrent and for basing cruise missiles in this country?

It may be that such statements are intended deliberately to misrepresent. It may well be the case that statements of the sort I've quoted so far are atypical or are allowed to pass unquestioned and unchallenged. But it may also be the case that these very same statements simultaneously exceed what was intended in their use and strengthen oppositional resolve – or even generate opposition in new quarters to which Edward Thompson's 'pre-modern means of communication' cannot reach. Even when the media seem to be operating at their most reactionary limits they may nevertheless promote courses of action quite contrary to any intended or hoped for.

I don't want to suggest for a moment that media stories about the preparations for a nuclear war, or about the movement opposed to these, can be taken up in any way that people fancy. Like any other stories, these come with a certain formal organisation; they make certain assumptions about who the consumers are, what their present knowledge is and what their views are. Frequently these assumptions are quite abstract, little more than a few aphorisms about 'ordinary people' or 'most folk'. But they still provide stories with a certain point of view and a certain structure that actual viewers and readers have to negotiate one way or another. They create a certain framework for viewers or readers, a framework that limits the available options. The accumulation of stories over time, the manner in which they have circulated and been consumed, creates a context of expectation for further stories on the same or a similar topic. This sediment of expectation also has to be dealt with.

Is it therefore possible to detect the adoption of a single, consistent point of view in these stories? Is there any difference between the so-called 'quality papers' and the 'popular' tabloids, or between the press and other media such as television? What is the character of the point or points of view adopted: is it such as to contribute to a 'pro' or 'anti' nuclear understanding? Does it promote actions at all, and if so of what kind? What can be done, if anything, to influence the point(s) of view adopted? These are some of the more detailed questions now to be considered.

For the most part I have referred to, and will be referring to, journalistic stories. To focus on them alone however would result in a quite artificially abstract discussion, for it would separate these journalistic stories from the contexts in which they are encountered – the viewing of an evening's television for example. In so doing the account could well lose sight of the potentially meaningful connections with other types of story that have been, and can be, made.

Take, for example, the charge of appeasement. Speaking at last year's Tory conference John Nott asserted that peace campaigners would 'emasculate our defences and adopt a policy of craven appeasement to the Soviet Union'. This was widely quoted in the press at the time and was again quoted some time later in *World in Action*'s programme about Edward Thompson. During the autumn and winter of 1981 ITV screened *The Wilderness Years,* a dramatic reconstruction of Churchill's life up to the outbreak of war in which the theme of appeasement was also touched upon. At this point you may well be thinking that I am about to read too much into this, that I am about to make connections where really none would be made. But consider the following letter published in the *Daily Express* (Oct. 29, 1981) under the headline 'Is it safe to ban the bomb?':

I would like to thank ITV for the 'Wilderness Years' and to congratulate Robert Hardy for his great portrayal of the late Sir Winston Churchill in the years between the wars. How easily people forget, and I only hope we never get into the same state again. Stay in power Margaret Thatcher and never disarm.

I am not suggesting a deliberate coincidence, merely a potential to make connections, a potential clearly realised by the writer of this letter.

Another respect in which context is important has to do with the use of the 'red scare' device. It is obvious that a considerable number of stories have been told in the last eighteen months where this device has been employed. Each seemingly 'new' development in nuclear policy is premised upon some reference to Soviet 'expansionism' or 'the Soviet threat'. Much has been said since the advent of the Reagan administration about the so-called 'window of vulnerability', about the apparent military advantage the Soviet Union possesses with its SS-20 missiles. On this Lawrence Freedman has commented that

Politicians found the SS-20 handy in returning Soviet propaganda, using this missile to suggest that the Russians had hardly been laggards in improving their own capabilities. The defence specialists became unhappy with the tendency to present NATO's own moves towards improving its nuclear forces as merely a response to Soviet moves. The case for this modernisation stood on its own merits because of real strategic needs, they insisted, irrespective of any Soviet activity. They became anxious lest a serious concession by the Soviet Union on its own SS-20s would put the NATO programme in jeopardy.[6]

But the politicians have not been notably deterred. This is because defence specialists, like Lawrence Freedman, may not appreciate the full semiological richness of the device in question. Used as a premise it removes the initiative from 'us', and places it squarely on 'them'. 'They' are positioned as the aggressors, 'we' merely respond to their clearly hostile initiatives in an attempt to deter. Moreover, those who employ the device do so with considerable confidence, for they can assume that many people will also believe that the Soviet Union is the aggressor and that 'communism' could well prove to be a fate worse than death.

In the aftermath of the demonstration of October 24, 1981 we find a number of newspaper articles employing the 'red scare' tactic. The report in the *Sunday Telegraph* (Oct. 25, 1981) made much of the presence of a Soviet camera crew at the demonstration. It also devoted several paragraphs to the funding of the demonstration, and in that context noted that Dr Joseph Luns, NATO Secretary General, 'estimated that Russia spent almost $6,000,000 (note not £6m, for the chosen form *visually enhances* the amount) in Western Europe last year'. No direct connection is made explicit; the co-existence of the statements is sufficient to imply a link. It then also noted that 'ten of the forty seats on the CND national council are now occupied by members of the Communist Party' – say no more, know what I mean...

It was clear from Paul Johnson's article in the *Daily Mail* (Oct. 26, 1981) that he hadn't wasted his time turning up to watch the demonstration on Saturday. (Just in passing, most of the reports in the papers made a point of saying that they *had* watched the demonstration.) No, he had spent his weekend absorbed in historical research to show that 'time and again the British electorate voting as a whole had emphatically rejected pacifism'. In the course of this carefully researched article he asserted that 'there is nothing more volatile than a carefully organised crowd'. And who 'carefully organised' that crowd? Was it perhaps the hundreds of policemen who, in the *Sunday Express* (Oct. 25, 1981) were said to have been 'tied up controlling the crowd'? No, of course not. Rather it was that 'a great deal of hard work, by large numbers of dedicated organisers – assisted by all the resources of the International Communist movement – went into collecting these crowds'.

What is clear is that these papers – the *Sunday Telegraph*, *Sunday Express*, *Daily Telegraph* and *Daily Mail* – have on this issue taken the initiative in playing the 'red-scare-communist-plot' trick. The BBC has not been slow off the mark either. Like these papers it was careful to point out, visually and verbally, the presence of anarchists 'hurling abuse'. A number of other accounts, including ITN's, managed not a whisper of their presence. And this initiative has come to provide a backdrop for subsequent stories. For instance, in *Nationwide*'s first of two reports on CND (Feb. 9, 1982), considerable emphasis was placed on the presence of Communist Party members in CND. Following an observation by Bruce Kent that CND was not in receipt of funds from any source whatsoever apart from individual donations in the form of membership subscription, this voice-over was delivered:

He refers of course to recent allegations that CND receives funds from Russia and has been infiltrated by Communists. Said Defence Under-Secretary Geoffrey Patte, towards the end of last year: 'The skill of the Communists and of the far left lies in their ability to foster and support movements with large numbers of non-political people by playing on their legitimate anxieties'. The campaign, however, makes no bones about the fact that there are indeed some Communists among their number...

Why was so much time devoted to what is, after all, unfounded allegation, kept alive in no small measure by those newspapers already mentioned? One possibility is that the charge of 'communist infiltration' was pursued in order to allow the representatives from CND to 'clear themselves' and 'allay fears'. If so, then it was done in such a way as to keep those fears alive: the effect of the item was to suggest that CND really had been besmirched, that it really did have something to clear itself of. Why did the item not simply demonstrate that it was mere allegation, or that there was no 'charge' to answer, if the aim was to dispel 'fears'?

The necessity to create 'folk devils' – monsters from a dark and dangerous world 'out there' on whom blame can be placed in situations like this – is not something that we can pursue here.[7] However, it is worth noting that 'communism' has long been employed in this way. It is a 'threat' which has had considerable fictional fuelling: from films such as *Ninotchka* (1939), through a rash of 'anti-communist' films in the 50s and 60s that included *Whip Hand* (1951), *I was a Communist for the FBI* (1951), *The Angry Silence* (1960) and *The Manchurian Candidate* (1962), to the more recent 'spy' novels from writers like Deighton, Le Carre and Forsyth. All of this and more – the many passing references to communism and the Soviet Union in all sorts of fiction and entertainment – bolsters any single mobilisation of the Device. It is, and has become through frequent use, a deeply engrained theme that has considerable popular credibility. Indeed it is the continuous servicing of this device which has in recent years come to make some kind of nuclear confrontation with the Soviet Union seem inevitable. Attempts to undermine the device are few.[8]

In looking at these aspects of the stories, I have identified their most conservative features. Fortunately, this is only *one* aspect, and it must be put in the context of others. So what are they? Let's continue for the moment with the coverage of the demonstration.

At the time that I was monitoring how this had been dealt with by the press and television, I was slightly taken aback. I fully expected that the treatment it received in those papers mentioned above would be typical. But this was not altogether the case. Even these papers found it difficult to trot out the archetypal 'demo story': how many people (take the lowest estimate), what disruption and/or trouble did it cause, how many arrested, and as an optional extra a few words from the 'star speakers' (but definitely only if there's space or time left after reporting the trouble caused). Difficult, but they still had a good try. Nevertheless, the coverage marked something of a turning point.

CND stages biggest demo as 150,000 march in London

London's biggest ever march unites

250,000 say No to Reagan

Two body counts on the October 1981 CND demonstration.
Top, The Sunday Times; *bottom,* Morning Star.

The size of the demonstration caused the first wobble. Most outlets seemed in agreement that it had been 'one of the biggest ban-the-bomb demonstrations ever'/'Britain's biggest CND demo since the 60s'/even simply 'the biggest demonstration in years'. The lunchtime bulletin on BBC TV stated that 'tens of thousands of CND supporters have begun what is claimed to be one of the biggest anti-nuclear protests held in London in recent years'. By its tea-time bulletin 'thousands of CND supporters took part in one of the biggest anti-nuclear protests ever seen in Britain. The size exceeded even the hopes of the organisers. According to the police, about 150,000 marched...' Only later was it said (in the context of a voice-over) that 'according to CND the crowd was more than a quarter of a million strong'. Elsewhere there was the usual 'claim' by the organisers set against 'official'/'police' figures. In addition to this several also chose to mention, as in the ITN bulletins, that 'CND has grown ten-fold in the past eighteen months' and that

CND 'now have strong allies throughout Europe capable of mustering the quarter of a million people who demonstrated in Bonn recently'. By the usual standards of demo reports, the inclusion of such 'hard numbers' was uncommonly generous.

This was coupled with a sense that a new or quite different kind of CND was being witnessed. In *The Sunday Times* readers were presented with a CND that had 'finally dispensed with its old middle-class Wood Folk (sic) image'. R.H. Greenfield in the *Sunday Telegraph*, watching the demonstration go by, found that 'CND is different now. Bigger, more slickly organised and less folksy, but perhaps less fervent too'. Across the mainstream journalistic spectrum there were many references to the presence of young people on the demonstration. In *The Guardian* on Monday it was said that Nick Davies had joined 'the punks, anarchists and their elders' – though from the rest of the report it sounds as though Davies was yet another to be 'looking on', to be an 'interested by-stander' at the start of the demonstration. The BBC's news bulletins also mentioned the 'young', though it was going out on its own when it said several times (over a shot of a young woman standing beside a grey-haired man) that 'the marchers were mostly young and had come from all over the British Isles'.

The Observer's demonstration was more in line with the others' when it said that it was composed of 'punks and grey-haired nuns, toddlers and children in prams, trade unionists and young women with painted faces. There were poets against the bomb, scientists against nuclear arms, teachers for peace, architects for peace and women for life on earth'. ITN's main evening bulletin on the Saturday evening summed up this sense of difference when it said that 'the most striking thing was the huge variety of people, from all over the country, from many different walks of life'. This had been immediately preceded by the remark that 'from the applause he (Tony Benn) got you might think it was a day dominated by the left, but...' – as if to suggest only those identified by ITN as 'the left' could possibly find anything Benn said worthy of applause.

This remark also emphasises something else. First it should be noted that once again we see, albeit in modified form, the employment of the 'red scare' device. It is employed in such a way, however, as to highlight the *popularity* of the demonstration. Taken together, the evidence of size and of composition – evidence that most stories included – was considered sufficient to suggest nothing less than 'a growing body of public opinion, strongly anti-American' (ITN). Though not always said in exactly these words, in one way or another this was a judgement acknowledged across the range – and even when the stories then went on to suggest that people were being misled, were well-meaning, idealistic, but really just down-right unrealistic. But the inclusion of such concessionary terms as 'well meaning', 'well intentioned' and 'idealistic' is still important. Such terms need not have been used.

Yet even though CND became during that weekend to be per-ceived and publicised as a popular movement, it did not and still has not really become one of the representative and quotable voices of Public Opinion. During the reporting very little was said about why the demonstration was being held. On the BBC's bulletins it was said that 'the CND had wanted the rally to be a demonstration of the tensions in this country about nuclear weapons' and that 'the organisers wanted a festival atmosphere... to be in keeping with the aim that unites them − for a globe free from nuclear weapons'. One suspects, however, that at least the second remark was there only because they had managed to shoot some footage of the globe that was bounced along on the demonstration. For the most part any-thing approaching statements of aims and objectives were sought from the 'stars' − the political 'stars' in the main, particularly Michael Foot and Tony Benn, who were by far the most frequently quoted.

By the end of the following week, despite the fact that this was a week of action throughout Europe, the organised peace movements had slipped back to near invisibility. Much of the reporting during that week shifted to focus on the reactions of governing parties, as expressed by figures like Lord Carrington, George Bush and Caspar

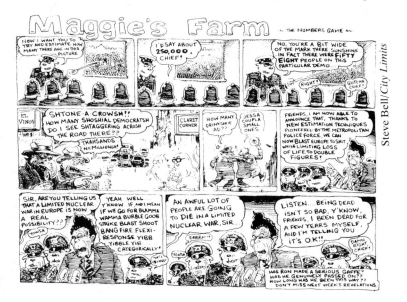

Weinberger. *The Sun* (Oct. 29, 1981) in one of only three references to the issue in a two-week period (*The Times, Telegraph* and *Guardian* had virtually daily coverage over the same period) praised what it called Lord Carrington's 'well reasoned' speech against 'the yearning... for an end to the wasteful arms race'. Or, as in *The Daily Telegraph,* attention began again to shift to what the 'baddies' were up to. On the same day it (alone) asserted that 'Russia had been quick to exploit the diplomatic and propaganda opportunities presented by last weekend's massive demonstrations...' Then, during the following week it picked up a speech by Helmut Kohl, leader of the West German Conservative opposition, and quoted him as saying that 'peace through disarmament was an illusion and impossible outside the Atlantic Alliance' (Nov. 6, 1981).

As to the relative status of the forces participating in these stories, there are a number of points to be made, but the main one is that despite its reported popularity the peace movement is only rarely placed as a source capable of defining the issues. Most of the time this is done by *official* sources – defence experts, politicians and the military. It would also seem that while the peace movement is worthy and has emotion and morality on its side, the advocates of militarism frequently have reason on theirs. So, why do I suggest that the reporting of the October 1981 demonstration was a kind of watershed?

I do not think that who gets quoted is the only evidence that we can or should go on, and if we look to other evidence we find that the picture is somewhat different. I think it is particularly true of papers like *The Times* and *The Guardian,* and especially of TV current affairs programmes, that they have mounted investigations which are at some critical distance from the official accounts. That critical distance is established by adopting at least some of the points of view that have been proposed in the peace movement – though this is only rarely acknowledged. By asking questions which take these points of view as premises, they are conferred some kind of authority – not an absolute one, but authority nonetheless. Then again, even in granting that the peace movement may well have morality on its side, these media can further enhance its authority.

The more that the American administration and the British government have to reveal about their nuclear plans, the more critical it seems that journalism has become. Much of the reporting since the end of the last year (1981) until now has been taken up with questions about the *cost* of 'modernisation'. The most recent example on television of this was *World in Action*'s 'The Price of Britain's Bomb' (Jan. 11, 1982). This opened with an account of Britain's Chevaline project – the attempt to produce an 'independent deterrent' capable of devastating Moscow. The main point was the massive escalation in the real cost of this project, and the initial, possibly deliberate under-estimation of costs. It then, on this basis, went on to discuss the possible costs of Trident I, which David Greenwood of the University of Aberdeen said could go as high as £10 million. The government's most recent estimate of Trident II, the more expensive option, has since been reported as much less than this figure.

Yet another strand of criticism has been the questioning of the supposition that a nuclear war can be limited, that is to say can be contained to a conflict within Europe. Invariably when this has been raised, various 'accredited witnesses' have been wheeled on to suggest that there can be little possibility of such a war being limited. Not least among these witnesses has been President Brezhnev himself; he has been frequently quoted as saying that any supposedly limited strategy is a fiction, for any nuclear strike would quickly escalate to all-out inter-continental war.

None of this, to be sure, is actively pro-CND. It can hardly be thought of as promotional material for the peace movement. For a start, in most of the reporting over the last eighteen months to two years the organised peace movement has been largely invisible. When it became more manifestly visible during the build up to, and in the aftermath of, the October demonstration the coverage was hardly unequivocally sympathetic. On the one hand all the now quite familiar stigmatisation devices were employed yet again, while on the other CND was billed as a growing and popular movement. So at best, the specific references to CND were, and are, paradoxical and contradictory. And certainly no-one has been seen or heard advocating membership of that or any other peace organisation.

But while it can by no means be said that the media have operated as an advertising agency for CND and the other organised peace movements, neither have they operated explicitly and systematically against them. What they have done is to *de-stabilise* the authority of the case for 'modernisation'. If in defence circles it was hoped that the modernisation of conventional, nuclear and chemical arsenals could be carried through quietly and with a minimum of fuss, then that hope has been thoroughly frustrated by the nosiness of at least certain sectors of the media – TV current affairs and the non-tabloid press especially.

It is true that many of those advocating the case for modernisation have not been stigmatised with quite the same vehemence that some have mustered for reporting the activities of CND. But they have been questioned, and pressed quite hard on other occasions.

President Reagan, Weinberger and Haig have been written and talked about in tones of measured concern — and sometimes in considerably stronger terms. As each episode has unfolded a questioning if not critical posture has been assumed. The reporting of both American and British defence policies has been such as to cast these as questionable. And the questioning that has taken place is not of the usual kind — that is, questions which permit those to whom they are directed to come back with *the* answers. Sometimes there have been questions which have been far from easy to answer.

Now I am sure that it can be argued of this account that I have overlooked this or that story which was undoubtedly anti-CND. I am sure that people will be able to produce examples which strongly suggest some conspiracy, or certainly some campaign to discredit CND in order to get what is perceived as a necessary modernisation of our 'independent nuclear deterrent'. However, such evidence would not disprove the case I have been attempting to make, which is that the stories being told are much more contradictory than these instances would suggest. Certainly there have been attempts to rubbish CND. But these must be set beside a whole series of TV programmes which have questioned the actions of the British and American governments, not to mention similarly oriented articles in at least some areas of the press.

It is certainly true that the media have not been quick to recommend or to campaign for actions which would establish the conditions under which nuclear disarmament (at least) could be achieved. Nevertheless, it does not follow from this that the media have contributed nothing at all in this respect. If they have done not a single other thing, they have surely put into question those who are in a position, and have been permitted, to define the issue. At the very least they have allowed military experts to state that the previously unthinkable is now not only thinkable but possible.

The open secret of the electronic media, the decisive political factor, which has been waiting, suppressed or crippled for its moment to come, is their mobilising power.[9]

This 'mobilising power' should not be under-estimated, as Edward Thompson and others appear to have done. Nor should it be seen as a power for the political-military establishment only. By allowing that establishment to state its case, often without question, it has furnished the opposition to nuclear arms with some powerful themes. In short the media have also contributed their mobilising powers to the organised opposition.

The defence correspondent

*Andrew Wilson**

Writing about defence for a newspaper, as I did for *The Observer* for sixteen years, you encounter two widely-held grounds for cynicism about your work. One is that defence correspondents are selectively fed secret information that does not reach the public, and thereby cajoled into purveying official views. The other is that they are denied access to vital facts, particularly about the deadliest strategic weapons systems, and are thus without the means of assessing what they hear and write about.

There may be some truth in both these suppositions (it would be wrong to generalise about the work of individuals), but the general effect can be exaggerated. In my own experience, the influences on the output of a defence correspondent, including, of course, the political character of his newspaper, are more subtle and varied.

Let us begin with the question of information. The amount of 'classified' information that reaches a journalist about such things as the precise range of a new battlefield weapons system or the number of civilians estimated to have 'died' in a nuclear field exercise, is small. There are possibly exceptions in the case of retired Service officers who become correspondents for reliable newspapers such as the *Daily Telegraph*. But the civilian defence correspondent, who normally comes from some other form of journalism, is treated, on secret matters, with considerable caution.

There is no 'positive vetting'[1] of defence correspondents. Editors simply tell the Ministry of Defence of their appointment, and the Ministry puts them on a list for invitations to off-the-record briefings and other facilities. The most important list, for invitations to high-level Whitehall briefings, includes representatives of all the national daily and Sunday papers (except the *Morning Star*), some weeklies such as *The Economist,* some technical publications such as *Flight International* and *Aviation Week,* and, of course, the BBC and ITN.

No Fleet Street journalist has ever been refused accreditation so

* *Andrew Wilson is an associate editor of* The Observer. *From 1963 to 1979 he was the paper's defence correspondent.*

far as I know, though there are clearly circumstances (for example if the journalist were thought to have hostile intelligence connections) in which it might happen. The Security Service (MI5) keeps a discreet contact with editors in case of such contingencies. It should be added that the briefings and facilities are, of course, a vital component of the defence correspondent's job. Without them he would become a mere armchair analyst, not normally what a newspaper wants.

When Britain was still 'East of Suez' the facilities offered by the MoD were very attractive, and not merely from the strictly professional point of view. Visits to Aden, the Gulf states, Singapore, Hong Kong, even Australia, were available for the asking, provided one didn't mind spending up to 48 hours in a C-130 cargo plane and was prepared to turn in 1,500-2,000 words on some part of the Services' function.

Today's visits to the Rhine army or RAF Germany are much less glamorous, but they are still vital if the defence correspondent is not to become desk-bound. This is particularly so for writers on 'popular' newspapers who, to get their paragraphs past hard-nosed news editors, have got to appear constantly 'on the job'. The power to withhold or minimise such facilities to a correspondent is a very powerful weapon in the hands of the Ministry, which, if it chooses, can use it to make an unwelcome journalist useless to his employer and so oust him from his specialised job.

In terms of 'copy', Whitehall briefings are generally more important than 'tour' facilities. But a distinction exists between collective briefings, typically given when major decisions are impending and have to be 'sold' to parliament and the public, and individual briefings, ranging upwards to interviews with the Secretary of State, for which special application is required (or for which the journalist may be invited to call in). Both types of briefing offer a means of springing 'leaks', but only the latter can provide the leak most sought after by the journalist, i.e. the 'scoop'. Here is a situation in which even quite well-regarded correspondents may find themselves at a disadvantage if they are thought unreceptive to what the Minister, or the Ministry, wants to put across to the public.

The fact that the information given in the highest-level briefings is often political rather than technical in no way devalues it. This is well appreciated by Warsaw Pact military attaches in London, from whom, sooner or later, any defence correspondent is likely to receive a tireless, and tiresome, series of social invitations. If he is wise, he will report these to the MoD, which in turn informs the Security Service – a predictable precaution in view of the unremitting intelligence war. But the correspondent, of any persuasion, who wishes to stay professionally 'clean', must then be ready to resist the possible follow-up, namely an invitation to co-operate with the intelligence authorities in providing his contacts with an item of 'disinformation' at the appropriate moment.

Clearly no serious defence correspondent works solely on the basis of briefings. Nor is any serious correspondent, however much in sympathy with the present general direction of Western defence policy, likely to accept uncritically much of what is put to him (or her). Even the most 'loyal' and conservative is bound frequently to criticise official policy on military-technical grounds, for example cost-efficiency of programmes and development projects. But it is here worth noting a process that operates in all successful PR.

Abu

By and large the officers and civilian officials appointed by the MoD to have contact with the media are carefully chosen. Some, at the higher levels, are extremely good and stimulating company. Friendships develop that can, and are intended to, play a significant part in the defence writer's general philosophy on defence matters. This tendency is unlikely to be corrected unless defence journalists are drawn into debates that extend beyond the mere technicalities of, say, how to find 'substitutes' for Trident.

The most rigorous forum for discussion of defence matters, the International Institute for Strategic Studies, is unfortunately almost wholly concerned with 'technicalities' in this sense, though it has never, to my knowledge, chauvinistically refused to debate alternative views with outsiders. Another resort of serious defence correspondents, when it touches their field, is the Royal Institute of International Affairs (Chatham House). It, too, is the prisoner of what might be called 'Alliance' philosophy. The third organisation frequented by defence correspondents, the Royal United Services Institute for Defence Studies, is totally so confined.

The only hope of changing this situation seems to lie with the efforts of a small number of university faculties and 'peace study' groups to involve working defence correspondents in their discussion of alternatives to a nuclear-based defence policy and (by implication) alternatives to the Alliance system of international security.

For some time now academic institutions have assumed responsibility for assembling and publishing a mass of precise technical information that, it could be argued, should have been gathered and presented by defence journalists. As a result, there is now little shortage of what might formerly have been called 'secret' information — about payloads, radiation effects, terminal accuracy and deployment patterns — on which to base a realistic discussion of the nuclear question. The danger, however, is that concentration on the technical aspects is liable, even among 'peace researchers', to obscure the question that, for me at least, lies at the heart of the nuclear debate. This is not a technical but an ethical question.

When, early last year, I came seriously to question my own long-held, if sometimes reluctant and qualified, views about NATO nuclear doctrine, it was only partly as a result of my long involvement in the technical-military debate. What that involvement *did* do was to persuade me that with the formalised adoption by NATO of a nuclear war-fighting strategy, the old fear of an all-out exchange was no longer a guarantee against resort to nuclear weapons on the battlefield. At the same time, the near-certainty of escalation (long recognised in Soviet defence doctrine, and till recently in NATO's) made the all-out exchange a real possibility for the first time since the early 1960's.

My awareness of the immorality of nuclear war (for which, of course, one must read nuclear planning) began much earlier, and stemmed, as I suppose must most people's, from the memory of Hiroshima. This was sharpened in my case by reading, some years ago, Masuji Ibuse's great Japanese novel 'Black Rain'. The essential quality of Ibuse's book is that it particularises the experiences of a small group of people in the Hiroshima holocaust in a way that overcame the, to me, deadening effect of endlessly repeated statistics.

As I explained in an article in *The Observer*,[2] my change of views was further advanced by my frequent confrontation, as a defence correspondent, with items of nuclear hardware, and more particularly the people who operate them. This was not — and it bears repeating — because such people very often correspond with the caricatures drawn by much 'peace' propaganda. (In the British services, at any rate, I found many of them moved by the same instincts that I was, but believing — albeit with growing difficulty —

that they would never be called on to 'press the button'.) Rather it was because I recognised that this very 'decency', like the technical fascination of the hardware itself, provided the essential framework within which to pursue peace-time planning for operations involving the death of millions.

My conviction is that however much I might not wish to undergo the consequences of a nuclear attack on this country (or the perhaps no less deadly consequences of a more distant exchange) I would find it even harder – indeed intolerable – to live with the responsibility for having unleashed such an event on other people. In short, I would not want to press the button, even in retaliation. Anyone holding this conviction, and believing, as I do now, that the occasion for 'pressing the button' may indeed arise, must in honesty cease to support the doctrine of 'deterrence'.

I remain as aware as ever of the problems that this raises in terms of our defence. But it does strike me forcibly that discussion of these questions must begin with recognition of what we cannot morally do, and proceed from that point onwards. We cannot argue backward to the point at which we find ourselves pledged, and irrevocably programmed, to commit the ultimate atrocity.

Censored:
the War Game story

*Michael Tracey**

In 1965, Hugh Carleton Greene had been Director General of the BBC for five years and was at the peak of his career. His Corporation towered over the national landscape − alive, confident, exciting, dominating with its wit and excellence. In drama, current affairs, comedy and religion his producers had started a cultural hurricane, and at the eye of the storm was Greene − Carleton Towers as *Private Eye* called him (on account of his height) − with his mission of liberalising the BBC apparently fulfilled.

Greene's success depended very much on the relationship he had established with the Board of Governors, and in particular with the two chairmen under whom he served, Arthur Fforde and Lord Normanbrook. But he also held strong personal views, in particular about the television audience's ability to form its own judgments on new ideas and on the broadcaster's position in promoting those ideas. In February, 1965 he made the definitive address of his career on these subjects:[1]

Censorship to my mind is the more to be condemned when we remember that, historically, the greatest risks have attached to the maintenance of what is right and honourable and true. Truth for ever on the scaffold, wrong for ever on the throne. Honourable men who venture to be different, to move ahead of − or even against − the general trend of public feeling, with sincere conviction and with the intention of enlarging the understanding of our society and its problems, may well feel the scourge of public hostility many times over before their worth is recognised. I see it as the clear duty of a public service broadcasting organisation to stand firm against attempts to decry sincerity and vision, whether in the field of public affairs or in the less easily judged world of the arts, including the dramatic art. I believe that broadcasters have a duty not to be diverted by arguments in favour of what

* Michael Tracey prepared this account while working as a Research Associate at the University of Leicester's Centre for Mass Communications Research. It is taken from the report he submitted to CMCR. He has also just completed a biography of Sir Hugh Greene, to be published by Bodley Head.

is, in fact, disguised censorship. I believe we have a duty to take account of the changes in society, to be ahead of public opinion, rather than always to wait upon it. I believe that great broadcasting organisations, with their immense powers of patronage for writers and artists, should not neglect to cultivate young writers who may by many be considered 'too advanced' or 'shocking'.

He then went on to talk about the audience, to accept that the TV enters every home:

We must rely, therefore, not only on our own disciplines, but on those which have to be exercised by, among others, parents. But programme plans must to my mind be made on the assumption that the audience is capable of reasonable behaviour, and of the exercise of intelligence — and of choice. No other basis will meet the needs of the situation... it would seem to me that no subject — no subject whatever — can be excluded from the range of broadcasting simply for being what it is. The questions which we must face are those of identifying the times and the circumstances in which we may expect to find the intended audience for a given programme.[2]

Greene could not work alone. He had to have behind him the body which constitutionally *is* the BBC, the Governors. More than anything else, though, he needed the support of the Chairman, and the chain-links which held Greene and his chairmen together were like all chains, capable of both supporting and binding. With Fforde they had supported, with Normanbrook the transition to bondage began. The Chairman became more intrusive, more perplexed and worried with the direction of the BBC — with its youthfulness, its occasional abrasiveness, its occasional sensuality and its persistent controversy. How far, Normanbrook asked, could the BBC go, where did its loyalties lie, to whom or what was it responsible, who or what should define its values, with whose world should it be in step? One particular decision was to provide some of the answers to those questions.

Announcement of the ban

On November 24, 1965 the BBC announced in a press release that it had 'decided that it will not broadcast *The War Game*, a film on the effects of nuclear war in Britain, made by Peter Watkins'. Anticipating the arguments which were about to burst, and continue to burst, about its corporate ears, it went on to add that 'this is the BBC's own decision. It has been taken after a good deal of thought and discussion, but not as a result of outside pressure of any kind.' The basic rationale for the banning of the film was, in the light of what had happened in the previous five years, curious: '...the effect of the film has been judged by the BBC to be too horrifying for the medium of broadcasting.' Somehow, as an argument emanating from Hugh Greene's BBC, that did not make sense.

Trying to establish the truth of how *The War Game* came not to be shown is rather like recent developments in sub-atomic physics: the closer you get to depicting the substance of the matter, the more it seems to dissolve and defy apprehension. The correspondence about *The War Game* is unlike anything which had gone before in the Director Generalship of Hugh Greene. In February, 1966 Francis Noel-Baker MP was just one of many who wrote to the BBC asking that *The War Game* be shown. Hugh Greene replied to him in much the same way as to the others: 'Our decision not to show *The War Game* on TV is final. The trouble is that even with a late night showing and a suitable warning, one cannot guarantee that there would not be children, the very old, or the unbalanced in the audience who might be seriously disturbed.'[3]

To read this was a curious experience, since many of the hundreds of other letters sent out by Hugh Greene responding to complaints seemed to take a very different tack. For example, he replied to one complaint about a film called *I Am A Camera:* 'We do not regard any of our viewing hours as being "children's viewing hours", since our AR (audience research) studies show that the available audience included substantial numbers of adults. In any case, I doubt whether children would have been attracted to this film, whose subject matter would have been quite foreign to their interests.' More generally, he wrote on another occasion to Terence Higgins MP, some of whose constituents had complained about programmes 'scripted with degrading, if not corrupting dialogue or situations'. Greene replied:

We would not agree that any of our productions would fall within any such definition. But if, as I suspect, what they really mean is plays or other programmes of a controversial or sophisticated kind, about perhaps 'difficult' subjects which may not be to the taste of all viewers or may be unsuitable for youthful viewers, I think we already have gone most of the way to meet the point they have in mind.

We do this in one or more of at least three ways:—

i) We place such programmes after what we call our 'watershed' time (currently after the ending of the News Bulletin at 9.05pm) since we believe that after this period it is reasonable to assume a predominantly adult audience;

ii) We make clear the nature of the programme, and the background which may make it distasteful to some viewers, by advance articles in the Radio Times;

iii) In the case of particularly controversial or potentially horrifying material, we supplement these measures by a special announcement at the microphone before the programme, so that viewers who wish to do so, may have an opportunity to switch off or to an alternative programme.

Compare that reasoning with that in a letter to another MP, Charles Mapp, who had asked the BBC to show *The War Game* late at night: 'The problem about a late night showing accompanied by a warning of the type you suggest is that, after all the publicity the film has had, people with neurotic tendencies might be encouraged to watch rather than discouraged. Children too are not always under effective parental control.'[4] Only weeks before Lord Normanbrook himself had written to a viewer who complained about *Till Death Us Do Part* : 'The final responsibility for deciding whether children should watch such a programme, at whatever time it is placed, must rest with their parents.'[5]

There also seemed to be an excessive sensitivity about the whole issue, for instance when Allen Lane of Penguin was refused permission to publish *The War Game* in book form.[6] There was equally an un-Greene like piece of casuistry when he refused a request from Neil Marten MP for a copy of the script. This was despite the fact that the British Film Institute had already shown the film to MPs in the Commons and the existence of an agreement between the Commons and the BBC that the latter would supply MPs with scripts of individual broadcasts.

The press had seen the film and in large part concurred with the BBC's decision, though not always arguing from the same standpoint. *The Daily Telegraph, Daily Mail, Daily Express, Daily Mirror, Daily Sketch, Sun* and the London evenings all supported the decision not to show the film. *The Guardian* implied that it should be shown and *The Times* said it would not have caused an outcry if it had been made for the commercial cinema. Only *The Daily Worker* demanded a screening. Comment in the Sundays and serious weekly journals brought the proportion in favour of the BBC lower, though still leaving a clear majority *for* the decision to ban the film.

It is interesting to look at the press comments in more detail. *The Times* thought that it was 'strange that the BBC did not decide to handle such an important and relatively uncharted subject journalistically, with a documentary programme. The effect of treating it in a dramatic vein can only charge it with extra emotion...' But the paper's argument that it would have caused far less fuss if the film had been made for the cinema only sidestepped one of the principal questions raised by the episode – which was just what kinds of issue could public service broadcasting raise and in what ways. *The Daily Telegraph* argued 'it is not stuff to be viewed by every elderly person living alone or for even a few minutes by a child. On that ground alone the BBC was justified in its decision'. The *Daily Mirror* TV critic felt that 'after watching this forty-five-minute horror film, directed by 30-year-old Peter Watkins (he has since left the BBC), it is difficult to understand why the BBC bosses were 'reluctant' to keep it off the screen. The decision was unquestionably right. It could have been made without hesitation... One final thought: director Watkins completely overlooked one vital political fact... that the nuclear deterrent and the ensuing truce between America and Russia has prevented major war for nearly twenty years'. For the *Daily Mirror*, then, the core of the argument was the political issues raised, that Watkins was making a case against the prevailing orthodoxy with its image of the nuclear umbrella.

This political theme was taken up by the *Daily Express*, which announced that 'this monstrous misrepresentation so accurately mirrors the claims of the Campaign for Nuclear Disarmament that it is a mystery how the BBC was induced to put up £10,000 to make the film, which could more accurately be called "The C.N.D. Game"...' And in an astonishingly elitist view, the *Daily Sketch* thought the film 'propagandist and negative in its approach, politically calculated in its effect. What producer Peter Watkins has made here is not a film about the Bomb, but a plea to ban it. It is a powerful plea, that employs every trick in the book, but it is about as dispassionate and balanced as a party political broadcast in aid of the Campaign for Nuclear Disarmament... It excluded hope. In that I judge it to be irresponsible... The powers-that-be have been right to censor *The War Game* for it is a game to be played seriously and responsibly. It is better left to the powers-that-be than to Mr. Peter Watkins.'

Only The *Daily Worker* front page streamer shouted 'This film must be shown', and the editorial read: 'No wonder the Establishment wants to stop the film being widely shown. If several million people saw it, the campaign for banning nuclear weapons would receive an enormous impetus... This is why the television ban has been imposed. It is the millions who would be stirred to anger and to action that the BBC is concerned with, not the few nervous people who might watch it despite any warnings given'. Meanwhile, Kenneth Tynan in *The Observer* made the most emotional plea. '*The War Game* stirred me at a level deeper than panic or grief

So long as adequate warning is given to depressives and other victims of nervous illness, it should not only be televised but screened in cinemas, not just here but everywhere on earth, especially in countries that possess (or would like to possess) the bomb. In refusing to show it, the BBC is like a doctor withholding the truth from a patient who is suffering from a potentially fatal disease; silence may preclude panic, but it also precludes cure.'

Watkins' war

By all accounts Peter Watkins was a rare talent. The writer Milton Shulman tells a revealing story of the first time he met him. In 1961, Shulman was an executive at Granada Television, one of whose duties was to survey any original film offered to the company for possible transmission. One day a young amateur film-maker came to him with a film for viewing. Sceptical but patient Shulman went to the viewing theatre with the 26-year-old Watkins: 'Hardly had the images begun to flicker on the screen when I found myself riveted by this extraordinary example of documentary filming. It dealt with the last ten days of the Hungarian uprising against the Russians in 1956. In a corner of Budapest a small group of students and workers were seen defying the tanks and the artillery of the Russians until most of them were either killed or captured'.

The impact of Watkins' film on Shulman was, he felt, due to the 'utter realism with which it depicted the violence, the agony, the despair and the courage of those involved in the microcosm of a revolution. The shuddering film frames during moments of violent action indicated the use of hand held camera. The rough camera work, the crude lighting, the texture of the celluloid, the chaotic shots of fighting, tussling men had that quality of immediacy and involvement reminiscent of the work of cameramen covering the front line during the Second World War at places like Stalingrad and Arnhem. It could only have been shot on the spot'.[7] How, Shulman asked Watkins, had he managed to be in Budapest and to get the film out? The latter informed an increasingly incredulous Shulman that he had been nowhere near the backstreets of Budapest. The whole thing had been shot, using amateur actors, in Canterbury, Kent.

The film was called *Forgotten Faces,* and was destined never to be broadcast in its entirety on British TV. It was too confusing as a televisual form and it mixed up the genres in its hell-bent desire to say something which Watkins felt desperately needed to be said.

Watkins had in fact perceived a relationship between the passiv-

ity of mass man and a mass communications system bleached of all colour and stripped of all depth. In a 'Personal Statement' in *Cine-Tracts* he paints a grim picture of a world slipping into psychic and nuclear disaster, moving lemming-like towards the edge of the precipice of Armageddon, inner and outer worlds shattered. So vivid is his personal nightmare that the future is in the present, the events have already effectively happened, all that is required is for them to be realised: 'Countless millions of those who will suffer will have had little if any knowledge about the nature and implications of the weapons that have caused the suffering, or about the social and economic and military and political forces and doctrines that have led to the war (i.e. World War III). In other words, though we have heard and read in the media about the possibility of nuclear war, most of us — including those in the media who have produced the words — have only a vague comprehension as to what those words mean, in their full context. We sit, and the words slip past, meaningless'.

Asking why this is the case, Watkins comes up with two solutions: 'We can perhaps understand it, first, as a problem related directly to the withholding of information from the public. Secondly, as related to the yet uncharted effects of the highly structured and repetitive visual language system that TV uses to impart what "information" it does convey.' He then illustrates the 'suppression of information' by reference to his own rather tortured career in trying to deal televisually with the nuclear issue. In fact his career seems to stumble from one banning to the next, one recent example being the extraordinary timing of a decision about a film he proposed to make for the Canadian Broadcasting Corporation. The film would have shown what could happen if a newly constructed reactor in the Philippines, partly fuelled by Canadian uranium, went into melt down. But the CBC abruptly withdrew its offer of work, and the letter confirming their rejection was typed only two days before the Harrisburg incident in the United States.

Watkins is clearly a dissillusioned and rather bitter man, but notwithstanding that his career raises some sharp points. He himself describes it in this way:

It is obvious, in fact, that the 'liberal' repression which has been emerging as a phenomenon in TV over the past 15 years is now fully out in the open, and that what one has to fear is not only the conservatism and political timidity at the managerial level but a particular kind of jealousy (of commitment) that cuts in from the ranks of one's own radical colleagues... using the names of 'quality' and 'professionalism' and 'objectivity' and 'standard', the middle echelon of Western TV are now exercising a repression which is even more severe than that of the political bosses who they like to claim are responsible, but in fact whose only guilt — often — is that they (the bosses) provide an excuse, or a front, for the middle echelon to carry out a wave of censorship (and self-censorship) unparalleled since the inception of public tv broadcasting. The result: that personal, subjective, committed, individual programme or film making is being openly stamped out, in the name of, and for the sake of, 'authoritative' and 'objective' programming. In a word, personal propaganda is being eliminated for the sake of corporate propaganda, quite oblivious of the fact that the effect (on the audience) of the highly structured, fragmented and repetitive language-system developed by TV has rendered the concept of 'objectivity' both absurd and, at the same time, highly dangerous. But, oblivious to this, Western TV is desperately pursuing its goal of safe, non-controversial 'quality' wrapped within a facile, narrative structure and quite ruthlessly eliminating everything which threatens this 'ideal'.[8]

This belief in the web of mystery and ignorance spun by the ubiquitous TV is not a product of Watkins' recent thinking. In the autumn of 1965 he was interviewed by James Blue and Michael Gill for the magazine *Film Comment*. Decrying once more the ignorance of the nation about the nuclear threat, and declaring his own intention in *The War Game* to try and relieve the population of the burden of that ignorance, he said: 'It's not so much that facts are deliberately withheld from people as there being a gentleman's agreement not to tell people – and this is why my film *The War Game* will really curl the eyeballs of a lot of higher ups. They will have to decide that it is not right for people to know these things because "this will affect the war morale of Britain", and that's going to be a hell of a thing to decide'.[9] His argument then is quite simple: people have a right to know and it is the duty of the programme maker to provide them with the roots of that knowledge. *The War Game* is a classic example of the working out of the process he is describing and experiencing, and for him, the more eyeballs that curl the better.

The establishment roused

Watkins had first come to the attention of Grace Wyndham Goldie, the influential BBC Head of Talks, as a 'brilliant young film editor who was obviously very, very talented'.[10] She and Huw Wheldon were both impressed by his work and were keen to keep him, even though they realised that he might be difficult. Watkins went to her one day and said that there was one programme he wanted to do and that was a film, using actors, about the effect on the population of an atomic attack. She said: 'How do you know what it will be like?' and recalls that he replied that she would just have to wait and see. Goldie was neither for nor against such a programme but wanted him to get something under his belt before attempting it. He went away and, much to her relief, came back with the idea of doing a film about the battle of Culloden.

Culloden, which depended a lot on authenticity of costume, eventually worked out at twice its original budget, and the BBC management took some convincing that they should fund this young man for a costly documentary — especially when his only real experience in the BBC was as a film editor on a programme about Tito. Both Goldie and Wheldon felt that their necks were on the block, but Wheldon called her one day to go and look at the rough cut. She saw it and immediately recognised it as a 'masterpiece', a watershed against which all other historical documentaries would have to be measured.

His talent finally recognised, Watkins was allowed to proceed with his original idea, and in the autumn of 1963 he formally proposed that he make an imaginative reconstruction of the impact of a nuclear attack on Britain.[11] Watkins was then a production assistant in the Documentary Department of Talks and his boss, to whom the proposal had been put, was Huw Wheldon. At the end of December, Wheldon commended the proposal to Kenneth Adam, Director of Television: 'Other factors apart I am anxious to keep Watkins; and to do so I must certainly let him get this film out of his system,' he wrote, and went on:

I have discussed this several times with H.T.G. Tel. (Grace Wyndham Goldie) who thinks that the film should be made on the grounds that, so long as there is no security risk and the facts are authentic, the people should be trusted with the truth. There are views at experienced levels that since nothing can be done to save Britain from annihilation, it is better not to portray such probable occurrences or to give frightening facts. She does not agree with this attitude, but notes that the film is bound to be horrifying and unpopular — but surely necessary. Major scientists seem to be those most concerned that the world should not be blind-folded in this matter...

Wheldon was, he said, not making the recommendation without 'the greatest anxiety' and admitted that anyhow the decision about the programme could only be made once they had had a chance to see it. Some of the doubts within the Corporation were not just about the likely content of the programme, however, but the way in which that content was likely to be shaped by Peter Watkins' obsession with the subject of violence: his training exercise, for example, had been about torture, not the usual sort of first time effort subject matter.

During research for the film, Watkins went to see Peter Thorneycroft, the Shadow Minister of Defence. Thorneycroft, though impressed by Watkins' enthusiasm and ability, was clearly worried about the film, and wrote to Greene on January 18, 1965 saying that the DG should give the programme his personal attention. Watkins had also approached the Home Office for information on the effects of nuclear attack and the preparations being made to meet them. In all he put 40 questions, most of which the

Home Office declined to answer on the grounds of security. The
Home Office then also expressed their hope that the supervision of
the programme would rest at the highest levels. Their concern was
expressed to H.D. Winther, the member of the BBC's administration with whom the Home Office liased, and in turn Winther
informed his chief, the Director of Administration, John Arkell.[12]

The seismometer in Wheldon's head had picked up the tremors
and he suggested to Adam that the Director General, Hugh
Greene, should view the script. He presented Adam with the
possible options:

... Once the script is available, we can decide (i) To call it off altogether. I
hope not, but obviously this will be possible; (ii) To ask the Chairman to
read it; (iii) To ask others (and they exist) to advise; (iv) To show it, without,
as D.A. says, 'compromising our independence' to Home Office officials;
(v) To move into the filming stage. This is what I hope will prove possible,
bearing in mind that the editing stage will involve the crucial decisions.

John Arkell was in favour of a Home Office official being
involved in the whole process of making the programme. Wheldon
disagreed and thought that if necessary they should show an
assembly of the programme to 'special people' including, possibly,
representatives of the Home Office, while making it clear that this
was not an advanced showing, rather a way of gaining advice. He
argued: 'An assembly, in our terms, is in no sense an "advance
showing". Programmes can be modified, altered, developed
beyond recognition according to decisions taken at a first assembly.
Being film, and not live studio transmission, it is entirely under
control at all stages i.e. the two crucial control stages are 1. script, 2.
assembly...'[13]

A briefing for Whitehall

By the autumn of 1965, the film had finally been made, and on
September 6, Kenneth Adam informed the Television Controllers
Meeting that the DG had viewed *The War Game* with the
Chairman:

...D. Tel. said DG had viewed 'The War Game' with the Chairman. They
had both agreed that it had been an impressive documentary, but had felt
that the responsibility for its public showing was too great for the BBC to
bear alone. The Chairman therefore proposed to take soundings in Whitehall from senior civil servants, probably including officials of the Ministry of
Defence. D. Tel. wished to make clear that these decisions had been taken

before, and therefore without any reference to, the report that Mrs. White-house had written to the Prime Minister suggesting that the Home Office, and not the BBC, should be responsible for deciding whether the programme should be broadcast.

This is in itself a remarkable statement, since it seems to be saying that Greene and Normanbrook had decided that the BBC should share its editorial responsibilities with outside bodies, something with Oliver Whitley, Greene's Chief Assistant, has subsequently described as 'unique to this occasion'. But on September 7, there is another even more remarkable set of statements. For Lord Normanbrook had been, before joining the BBC, Secretary to the Cabinet and head of the Civil Service, and he chose to discuss the film, and the 'problems' he felt flowed from it, with his successor, Sir Burke Trend:

The BBC have made a film for television, under the provisional title 'The War Game', which shows the consequences which might follow for the civil population if this country were subjected to a nuclear attack. This film is not designed as propaganda: it is intended as a purely factual statement, and is based on careful research into official material. I have seen the film, and I can say that it has been produced with considerable restraint. But the subject is, necessarily, alarming; and the showing of the film on television might well have a significant effect on public attitudes towards the policy of the nuclear deterrent. In these circumstances, I doubt whether the BBC ought alone to take the responsibility of deciding whether this film should be shown on television − or, if it is to be shown, of deciding when it should be put on. It seems to me that the Government should have an opportunity of expressing a view about this.

I should like, therefore, to suggest that, in the first instance the film should be seen by senior officials of the departments concerned...[14]

Lord Normanbrook's involvement in the questions surrounding the programme was also given added significance by the fact that Hugh Greene, the Director General, and with whom he had first seen the film, was now abroad. In his absence, a private showing of the film was arranged at Television Centre for Sir Burke Trend, Secretary to the Cabinet, Mr. W.I. McIndoe, his Private Secretary, Sir Charles Cunningham, from the Home Office, Mr. G. Leitch, from the Ministry of Defence, Brigadier A.C. Lewis, representing the Chiefs of Staff and Mr. A. Wolstencroft from the Post Office. From the BBC were Normanbrook, Robert Lusty, one of the Governors, John Arkell, the Director of Administration and Oliver Whitely, Chief Assistant to the DG. There then followed a discussion, the minute of which by Normanbrook reads:

After the showing of the film we had a short discussion about it. I began this by stating the case for showing such a film. The essence of this case was that the dialectical discussion of defence policy, and particularly of the policy of nuclear deterrent, was conducted on an abstract intellectual level, with little public appreciation of the practical realities involved; and that, if in a democracy the people were to take their proper share in influencing decisions on such policies, they ought to have a clearer imaginative picture of the realities of nuclear warfare. I put this case as forcibly as I could. I made it clear that I was not myself arguing that the film should be shown, either now or at some future date: I was concerned only to establish the fact that a case could be made for showing it – not for any sensational purpose, but as a matter of policy.

The officials agreed that this was the major question for decision; but they preferred to reserve judgment on it until they had been able to reflect and discuss it among themselves.

On less substantial points, some of them thought there were some inaccuracies in the film; but they agreed that these were such that they could be corrected if it were decided to show it.

On a more important point, most of them seemed to think that, in its concluding stages, the film ceased to be an objective statement and became somewhat tendentious – in the sense that it suggested that the risk of outbreak of nuclear warfare was increasing, and indeed becoming imminent, mainly by reason of the 'proliferation' as nuclear weapons were coming into the control of less responsible countries. If ever the film were to be shown some revision of the concluding sequence would need to be undertaken. Most of them also felt that, taken as a whole, the film would have the effect (whatever its intention) of lending support to the Campaign for Nuclear Disarmament.

The officials agreed however, that the major question of policy was whether it would be expedient, in the public interest, that any film of this kind should be shown on television. They undertook to address their minds to that question – leaving aside for the moment the problems of adjusting the film to meet the lesser difficulties to which they had drawn attention. I will arrange for Sir Burke Trend to keep me in touch with the progress of these discussions in Whitehall about this film.[15]

What do we have then? Normanbrook has been involved in discussions about the possible future of the film with civil servants concerned with Britain's nuclear policy at the very highest level. His central concern, as expressed in the letter to Burke Trend – 'the showing of the film on TV might well have a significant effect on public attitudes towards the policy of the nuclear deterrent' – is the same as theirs as recorded in his minute of their comments: 'The officials agreed... that the major question of policy was whether it

Advice from Protect and Survive *on what to do before the bomb drops:
a different picture from* The War Game.

would be expedient, in the public interest, that any film of this kind
should be shown on television'. At no point is the central question
that of the immediate psychological impact of its horror.

What did the other BBC representatives think? Robert Lusty,
the other Governor who had seen *The War Game,* felt that on the
whole it should not be shown.[16] Oliver Whitely thought it should,
and wrote a draft introductory statement to the programme which
he thought might alleviate some of the problems:

Peter Watkins, who made the programme, did so because he felt deeply
that people who live, as we do, under the shadow or under the protection –
however you prefer to put it – of the nuclear bomb; should have a realistic
idea of the probable effect on the population of the explosion of such a
bomb in the neighbourhood.

The BBC allowed him to make this film. On what basis could it be said
that it is wrong even to attempt to make a programme with this aim? It was
made clear that permission to make it did not carry with it a guarantee to
broadcast the film. That could only be decided when the film was finished
and could be judged after being seen.

The film was made and the decision taken, not easily, to broadcast it.
The film is a remarkable achievement by the producer and all who coopera-
ted with him. It isn't perfect. It isn't always fair. It has tried very hard to be
accurate. It is one man's conception and we have resisted the temptation to
fiddle with it to meet other men's preferences.[17]

By the beginning of November, however, those 'other men's
preferences' were emerging as the deciding factor in the fate of *The
War Game.* On November 5, 1965 Normanbrook had another
meeting with Trend, Cunningham and Wolstencroft. They reported

that the various Ministers had been informed about the film, did not themselves wish to see it, did not wish to express any opinion on whether it should be broadcast or not, and would leave the decision entirely to the BBC. He added: 'It is also clear that Whitehall will be relieved if we do not show it'.[18]

On November 22, Hugh Greene told the Board of Management that a decision was imminent,[19] and that Kenneth Adam had already drafted a statement for the Chairman. The final decision must have been made during the course of the next 48 hours, because on November 24, Normanbrook wrote to Burke Trend informing him that it had been decided not to show the film, enclosing a copy of the press release and adding that this would go out at 4.00pm on November 26.

Who made the decision?

The basic decision, then, not to show the film began to crystallise between November 5 and 24. Trying to find out precisely what happened during this period is fascinating if frustrating, because it is impossible to discover who made the specific decision and what the arguments for making it actually were. There is absolutely no written record, and whether it was Greene or Normanbrook, or both in tandem, they chose not to make any official record.

There were two meetings of the Governors during this period, but again there is no minute of there having been any discussion whatsoever about the impending decision. This does not mean that the Governors were not interested in the events. Glanmor Williams, who had just been appointed as the National Governor for Wales, recalls that after the Governors took note of the decision and endorsed it at their meeting on December 2, they demonstrated a lot of interest in their discussion and several actually asked to see the film. He *does* recall that Normanbrook was much firmer than Greene in wishing to stop the transmission of the programme, and that the reason for this was his concern that the programme would damage the national interest.[20]

The chief executive body of the BBC is the Board of Management (BOM), on which sit all the Corporation's most senior executives, with the Director General in the chair. In trying to find out whether or not and in what ways the programme was discussed by BOM I approached John Arkell, then the BBC's Director of Administration. He said that the decision not to show the film had been made by BOM and that he was in the chair. He couldn't remember the date but was quite adamant that that was what had happened. This was intriguing because up until then no one had suggested that BOM was involved to that extent. He further argued that when Greene returned from abroad and heard of the decision he was not best pleased, but then 'gallantly supported it'. The ground for the decision, he recalled, was the sheer horror of the film, with very little attention being paid to the policy aspects. Oliver Whitley, he thought, would probably have been given the task of informing the chairman. The only proviso Arkell allowed for was that BOM may have technically only recommended that the programme not be shown and that the final decision had been left to Normanbrook.

One possible scenario then is that the BOM made the decision on one basis, that is the question of horror, and that Normanbrook welcomed and endorsed the decision on another basis, that is the policy implications. Hugh Greene therefore returned to find himself faced with a fait accompli, which out of loyalty and tactics he had to support. He would clearly have realised that the issue would continue to wrankle and that therefore he would wish to be seen to have been the one who made such an important decision.

There is only one problem with this scenario, which rests very much on Arkell's memory, and that is that no one else seems to remember it that way and there is no record of it having been that way. At the one BOM meeting during this period when Greene was absent (at a European Broadcasting Union meeting in Germany), there is no minute of any discussion about *The War Game*. In fact, according to the minutes *The War Game* was not discussed at all by BOM from their meeting of October 18, when it was raised, to November 22, when Greene informed the meeting that a decision was imminent.[21]

Another member of that meeting at which Greene was absent (on November 15) discounts completely Arkell's version and added that Kenneth Adam, whose immediate responsibility the programme was, would have avoided bringing any decision to a BOM meeting with Arkell in the chair, mainly because the Output Directors on BOM, though they respected Arkell's administrative abilities, never had any confidence in his programme judgement. He also recalled that BOM never collectively saw the film, something which they would have insisted on if they had been asked to decide its fate.

Frank Gillard, then the BBC's highly respected Director of Sound Broadcasting — and a close confidante of Greene — remembered that Greene had made the decision. He remembered this in particular because he recollected that Greene was worried about it, continued to brood over it and said to Gillard on one occasion that he was not sure he had made the right decision, a sign of doubt which one certainly didn't associate with him. He was clearly worried, according to Gillard, about the effect this episode would have on his reputation as the champion of liberal programming policy.[22] In correspondence with the author, Gillard explained:

The one thing I am quite certain about is that BOM did not take the vital decision to ban 'The War Game'. BOM did not have that kind of role. Had such a decision been taken, it would of course have been recorded in the minutes. If it happened at all, this was purely an informational matter and as such would not have been recorded. Hugh Greene always spoke of the decision as one which he alone took. BOM's participation was negligible.

Curiously then, it is impossible to be definitive about the decision. The likeliest explanation is that there were two elements involved: one defined by Normanbrook's concerns, the other by Hugh Greene's perception of that concern combined with his own doubts about the programme. But there seems no question that Normanbrook was closely involved with the decision to ban *The War Game.* In all probability he was the deciding factor, and his reasons for banning it had nothing to do with anxiety about suicidal grannies.

It is not surprising that Lord Normanbrook should be concerned by the programme. In his pre-BBC career he had been a key part of the British political establishment, closely involved with the development of defence policy and with the activities of the intelligence agencies. For example, when, after the Profumo scandal in 1963, the Conservative government became nervous about security, Normanbrook was one of those asked to sit on the new Standing Commission on Security. When Sir John Masterson was writing his book on double agents, which he knew would need security clearance, he approached Normanbrook to see if this would be forthcoming because he was perfectly aware that Normanbrook, who was by then Chairman of the BBC, retained impeccable connections with the British intelligence community.[23] Normanbrook had also been head of the Civil Service and Chairman of the Home Office Defence Committee, which is at the heart of civil defence planning. Given this background, in which he had been one of the moulders of the post-war consensus on the virtues of the nuclear deterrent, he could not possibly allow Watkins' mould-breaking film to be shown.

Disarming
the disarmers

Ruth Sabey[*]

To the many thousands of men and women, of varying political persuasions and personal beliefs, who have become concerned about the impending possibility of nuclear war, their treatment in the media must at times seem astonishing. For their desire to see a world devoted to peace has often been presented by the press as 'unpatriotic', 'against the national interest', 'left-wing' and actively 'pro-Soviet'. Where it is obvious such labels do not apply, peace movement supporters are instead presented as 'naive', 'well-meaning', 'idealistic' or even 'mad' and 'hysterical'.

Last year (July 9, 1981), the *Colchester Evening Gazette* ran a front page article under the headline 'CND and the Russian Link'. Prominently juxtaposing the KGB and CND symbols, this purported to 'reveal' how the Russian state police had been 'trying to use the peace campaigners'. Factual details presented by reporter John Cleal, an ex-army officer, were sparse, and included the arrangement of 'peace trips' to the USSR and a propaganda effort aimed at schools, churches and trade unions. But the article – a blatant example of the type of 'smear' campaign some peace movement supporters had been fearing – proved something of a watershed. For it produced both a strong local response (numerous angry letters, a picket of the newspaper office and a formal union complaint against the reporter) and encouraged Mediawatch[1] to coordinate the collection of similar examples.

This account draws on some of those examples, but starts by examining the government's own anti-peace movement offensive and the use of the smear device during reporting of the 1981 CND march and rally in London.

* *Ruth Sabey is a teacher and coordinator of Mediawatch, a group set up to monitor press coverage of the nuclear issue and encourage improved access for peace groups.*

The Spring Offensive

Though not officially opened until March, 1981, the government's 'Spring Offensive' against the peace movement was previewed, like all good public relations exercises, in advance. *The Guardian* (Feb. 16, 1981) carried a report under the headline, 'Nott prepares spring offensive to counter CND successes' and examined the Defence Minister's proposal to launch a political and public relations campaign to justify nuclear 'deterrence'. Nott was said to be concerned that public anxiety about nuclear war, rather than expressing itself in support of government policy, had instead prompted a vigorous revival of CND.

At a public level, the Ministry of Defence campaign mostly involved the publication of a series of pamphlets and brochures. These range from a specific defence of the decision to accept cruise missiles in Europe to a number of 'fact sheets' about 'The Nuclear Balance', 'Arms Control', 'NATO' and 'Deterrence'. The information contained inside is pure NATO propaganda, invariably portraying the Soviet Union as both aggressive and militarily far superior to the Western allies. But some of the material is both slickly produced and clearly aimed to play on public fears. One leaflet, entitled 'A Nuclear Free Europe? Why it wouldn't work' shows that pushing the Russian SS 20s behind the Ural Mountains would still make us 'Target Europe'; another shows a grim-faced bulldog menaced by a giant bear under the title 'How To Deal With A Bully'. 'NATO's policy of deterrence has kept peace in Europe for over 30 years', it concludes. 'That's a history lesson none of us can afford to ignore'.

Not all the Ministry's propaganda has been aimed solely at CND. As part of the Defence White Paper of April, 1981, for instance, a 'nuclear essay' (written by deputy secretary Michael Quinlan) was published in order to set out the government's case for the British independent deterrent (*Observer*, April 19, 1981). The concern this time was in part with the Ministry itself, where the huge cost of Trident has been seen as a threat to other spending. Quinlan's treatise, according to *The Times* (April 24, 1981), was 'written in his distinctive, crisp style, a great improvement on the leaden prose that usually afflicts such documents', and argued again that, for all the horror of their power, nuclear weapons had kept the peace in Europe since 1945. Presumably the White Paper had its effect, since *The Times* (May 25, 1981) reported that the MoD was seeking the help of the academic community in its effort to ensure that the revived debate about nuclear weapons policy was conducted on 'an informed basis'.

EITHER SIDE OF THE URALS –
IT'S STILL TARGET EUROPE

Ministry of Defence propaganda:
how to deal with CND?

Most importantly, many of the press reports on these initiatives started with the assumption that the growing peace movement did not result from genuine concern with the government's defence policy, rather from a lack of understanding. It was therefore only reasonable that details of the policy should be made available in an 'informed' way which would lead to greater public acceptance of the need for nuclear weapons. How effective this has been, against the increasingly belligerent statements from the White House, is difficult to judge. But it is still true that no major national newspaper lends editorial support to unilateralism and that the views of the Campaign for Nuclear Disarmament remain on the periphery of the debate. Even *The Guardian*'s report of the 'Spring Offensive', for example, relegated the fact that on the same day a petition signed by 500,000 people was handed in at No. 10, Downing Street to a brief final reference. If evidence were needed of the 'vigorous revival' the paper had referred to earlier, that was it.

The Whitehall assault on CND has not abated, however, since the 'Spring Offensive'. On October 9, *The Times* carried a report under the headline 'Whitehall hits back at unilateral disarmers' and quoted Douglas Hurd, Minister of State at the Foreign Office. 'The Government has no intention of becoming a silent and passive target for criticism of its defence policy', Hurd said. 'It is our job to join in the debate and contribute a clear statement of the facts and of the reasoning which underlies what we do'. Hurd was also reported as saying that a weakening of Western Europe's will to maintain or enhance its military strength would reduce pressure for Soviet concessions in arms negotiations and increase the likelihood of Soviet arms expansion. This was because 'petitions and resolutions of the international community bounce off the Soviet government like paper darts aimed at an armoured giant'. Importantly, towards the end of the article the term 'unilateral disarmers' was replaced by 'pacifists', a term which strongly suggests negative views (particularly when associated with defence) and one that has been frequently used to label the peace movement as a whole.

The Times also continued this one-sided 'debate' on October 15, under the headline 'Unilateralism the enemy of disarmament', reporting that various delegates had expressed their views about those calling for unilateral disarmament during the defence debate at the Conservative Party Conference. G. Gollop (Bristol NW) described them as 'sincere ideologists... being exploited unashamedly by others for political purposes'. B. Leigh (Richmond) 'said he could reveal a fact which had not appeared in the newspapers, that the KGB had spent $100 million on an anti-neutron campaign in Western Europe', whilst Mrs. B. Utting (Portsmouth South) 'said

Mr Tony Benn and his left-footed followers were using CND to play on the natural fears of ordinary people...' At the same time, the Freedom Association's newspaper *The Free Nation* contained a special 'Conference News' insert with a 'profile' of Bruce Kent, general secretary of CND, which can only be described as a diatribe against the peace movement as a whole, and its Christian supporters in particular.

Such press reports apart, the Ministry itself has moved on to higher things than just pamphlets. In February, 1982 it announced the production of a film which would explain 'the official policy of nuclear deterrence', a clear response to the popularity of *The War Game*. Its expectation is that this will be shown to debating societies, Women's Institutes, environmental organisations and protest groups, as well as at commercial cinemas (a reasonable ambition since Ministry films often form the 'short film' part of cinema programmes). The film will also be shown in schools, where CND has found it particularly difficult to put its views across.

October 1981 – what the papers said

Reference has been made elsewhere (see 'Peace In Our Times?' by Ian Connell) to the press reports of the October, 1981 demonstration, when some 250,000 people showed their support for unilateral nuclear disarmament. But a closer examination of the coverage given in the national press over the period October 24-26 demonstrates the way in which such an event can be manipulated to suit editorial policy. To start with, the *Daily Express* and *Daily Telegraph* – with an estimated readership of over 3½ million[2] – carried advance news of the demonstration not as an item of interest in itself, but concentrating on the problems it would cause for police on alert for IRA bombers. *The Daily Telegraph* also covered speeches by Pym, former Defence Secretary, Edwards, Welsh Secretary, and a letter by Goodhew, vice-chairman of the Conservative backbench defence committee – all expressing concern that the government's defence policies were failing to retain popular support. However, the government was still 'sustaining a process of continuous explanation and representation of the philosophy and rationale of the concept of nuclear weapons for peace' (Pym quoted in *The Daily Telegraph*). *The Guardian* reported Pym as saying that the Soviet Union aimed for global domination and had played on the natural fears of the public in the West 'with an evil brilliance'.

The decision to use the IRA rather than unilateral nuclear disarmament as the central issue was also reflected in the *News of the World, Sunday Express* and *Sunday Telegraph* coverage of the event itself. Philip Wrack's column in the *News of the World* — estimated readership nearly 5 million — said: 'So, at a time when risk of IRA attack is high, why allow people like the CND to hold a massive demonstration? Yesterday's march tied up more than 1,000 policemen. No wonder the bombers keep getting away with it'. The *Sunday Express* leader — estimated readership over 3 million — announced: 'One senior police officer watching the solid stream of protestors piling into Hyde Park said "What happens if the IRA let off another bomb? We would be helpless. We couldn't move",' whilst the *Sunday Telegraph* front page declared: 'Thousands of police, including helicopter patrols, kept watch amid fears that the demonstration could provide cover for another IRA bomb out-rage...'

The *Sunday Telegraph* front and back page article was in fact a clear example of misinformation and innuendo. Not content to centre the report initially on the IRA, it then went on to raise questions as to how the demonstration was funded. 'Demonstrators travelled free in special trains and coaches from all parts of Britain and lunches were provided for leading campaigners and officials... Dr Joseph Luns, NATO Secretary-General, has estimated that Russia spent almost £6,000,000 on anti-nuclear propaganda in Western Europe last year. Ten of the 40 seats on the CND National Council are now occupied by members of the Communist Party while Trotskyists operate at the grass roots'. This resort to misin-formation was significant not only for its timing — when the Government's defence policy was increasingly being questioned — but the *Sunday Telegraph* also managed to totally ignore the alter-natives being presented by the peace movement. The paper's hope, no doubt, is that the more people see and hear the 'slur' that the KGB are financing the peace movement, the more they will come to believe it.

Coverage given by the dailies on October 26 itself also expressed 'concern' that growing support for the peace movement may unsettle the balance of East/West relations. The *Daily Telegraph* gave over considerable space to Julian Critchley, Conservative MP for Aldershot, whose headline declared: 'Whatever our naive demonstrators may think, military strength, not a disarming smile, is what keeps Russian hands off Western Europe'. The article itself, however, suggested that Critchley takes the views of the peace movement more seriously than the 'naive' label indicates. 'The arguments put forward by the peace movement are both subtle and sophisticated, and it will not be enough to mutter publicly about

Communist influence and exploitation — which do exist. The arguments have to be refuted'.

John Akass, in *The Sun*, said he thought that President Reagan probably accounted for part of CND's revival. 'His blurted remark about the possibility of a tactical nuclear war in Europe... has been seized upon by the disarmers as evidence of dotty and homicidal intent... All Ronald Reagan has done is say out loud what his fellow-Americans have been saying in private for decades...' Akass then went on to say how the CND revival was discomfitting for those like himself who dither somewhere in the middle of the argument. But even in dithering, he manages to continue the 'red slur': 'We ditherers would find it helpful too if the CND were more careful about the company it keeps. The movement was half killed by the communists and the Trotskyists in the 60s and it could easily happen again'.

And in case the politicians were in danger of being influenced by the democratic process of demonstrations, petitions, letters, festivals, meetings and other forms of peaceful (non-violent) action, they could turn to Paul Johnson in the *Daily Mail* for re-assurance. 'Those 150,000 people who crowded into Hyde Park at the weekend clamouring for unilateral disarmament will do little harm provided responsible politicians remain cool and leave it to the mob to get excited... there is nothing more deceptive than a carefully organised crowd. A great deal of hard work by large numbers of dedicated organisers (*and here is that 'slur' again*) — assisted by all the resources of the international Communist movement — went into collecting those crowds throughout Europe last week. There was nothing spontaneous about them'. Finally, the *Daily Express* opinion column portrayed the peace movement as 'mad', willing to risk Russian repression, and failing to see nuclear weapons as the foundation of peace. 'Suddenly and soberingly, a large number of people seem ready to risk a dark age of Russian repression', it concluded.

Examples from the local press

Local press coverage of the peace movement varies considerably — and is often dependent on the ability of local campaign groups to make contact with a sympathetic journalist or submit material acceptable to the editor. But many of the articles generated by local papers appear simply to restate the government's 'Protect and Survive' position on Civil Defence, giving advice on what to do in the event of a nuclear attack and with little more analysis than how and when to plant your potatoes!

Typical of this approach was the *Wisbech Standard* (Nov. 6, 1981), which carried a feature headed 'Millions expected to live' and explaining what arrangements were being made for after a nuclear attack. 'The local authorities would have the same responsibilities after and during a war as in peace time', the paper explained prosaically. 'They must gather intelligence from the military and deal with housing; sanitation; disposing of the dead; food distribution; requisitioning of labour...' Even so, under the headline 'No "emergency" help if you are in the blast area', it made clear that control of the media itself will also be priority: 'When a war is imminent both the BBC and Independent radio and television would provide information for the public... limited broadcasting would be available, so the BBC plan to operate one radio station'.

Whilst reporting such developments, local papers can still manage a dig at CND. The *Hexham Courant* (Nov. 20, 1981) carried a front page article about how an old 'cold store' building was being converted to a sub-regional centre of government for use in the event of nuclear war, and the editorial of the same date explained the difficult decision that had to be taken about whether or not to go ahead and publish the story: 'In the circumstances, it was almost impossible for any self-respecting newspaper simply to ignore the matter and, sensibly, the Home Office has taken the same view... It could, perhaps, have weilded the big stick and endeavoured to throw a security blanket around the whole operation... there will no doubt be howls of indignation from those whose hysterical reaction to the possible threat of nuclear war... is in itself doing not a little just at present to increase instability and tension in the world, and so make the dread possibility of nuclear conflict that much more likely'.

Some papers have deliberately gone on the offensive against CND. For example, the *Oxford Journal* (Aug. 7, 1981) carried an unsigned article (but with the authority of a sub-heading 'On the line to the lobby') called 'Belt up about the bomb!' This contained trivialisation in the extreme. Those who suffer from 'the all too prevalent urge to support the Campaign for Nuclear Disarmament, in the fond belief that somehow or other it will banish from our planet the menace of "the bomb"' were compared to people who don't wear seat belts, avoid risks to health by smoking or indulge in promiscuous sexual behaviour! But behind this was the more familiar argument that 'by threatening to use against Britain her overwhelming forces, the Russians could turn our country into an advanced base against the U.S. Instead of cruise missiles we could become a launching pad for Russian missiles', a theme also taken up by the *Birmingham Post*'s editorial (Nov. 3, 1981) where the question was posed: 'Have the CND et al ever considered the possibility that if Britain adopted unilateral nuclear disarmament, it might end up as a platform for Russian missiles deployed against the United States?' The answer of course is 'yes', and in the words of the much maligned Tony Benn: 'We will not accept the domination of this country by Russian Generals or American Generals or British Generals or the people who are preparing repressive measures in the name of Civil Defence backed up by the police with CS gas and plastic bullets...' (speech at Hyde Park rally, Oct. 24, 1981).

Even when local CND groups have been directly approached for their views, these haven't always been fairly reported. When the *Coventry Evening Telegraph*, for instance, followed up Earlsdon CND's suggestion for a nuclear free zone in Coventry, and other council initiatives, it was a small point about the banning of military displays from council-controlled land which got the headlines. 'Banish the bands says CND group' ran the eventual headline, over the story that military bands could be banished from the streets of Coventry. Other important issues barely received a mention.

It is true that newspapers can be encouraged to retract inaccurate statements, as happened with the *Sunday Telegraph* report of the 1981 CND march referred to earlier, or to provide a balance through the letters page, as happened with the *Oxford Journal* article. But rarely is information given on the quantity of letters received and how they are selected.

Newspaper editors will no doubt argue that they provide what people want and that what they want is reflected in circulation figures. But until the present structure of the press is changed, especially the increasing dominance of the national press by large UK conglomerates and foreign-based multinationals,[3] it is unlikely that this will be the sole factor involved. Meanwhile, the media's influence can be reduced not merely by highlighting inaccuracies and bias but by supporting and encouraging positive regional and local alternatives.

The ban that backfired

Michael Pentz*

'I am the very model of a safe Director-Gineral,
The water coursing through my veins is very largely mineral;
The way my powers are exercised, though more or less inscrutable,
Denotes an awful fear of things I deem to be unsuitable;
In controversial matters I display a certain latitude,
Except where the Establishment requires a kneeling attitude,
And while allowing programmes which are slightly on the bluey side,
I cannot think it wise to question universal suicide.

I draw the line at dissidents in matters academical,
Believing it disturbing to indulge in the polemical;
And if, instead of blessing war, a scientist should curse it, he
Will find the door is bolted at the Open University.'

Roger Woddis

The BBC has cancelled a lecture on nuclear arms by Professor Michael Pentz, dean of science at the Open University, on the grounds that it was 'inappropriate and unsuitable'.

(With acknowledgements to the New Statesman,
December 12, 1980)

The saga of the BBC television lecture that got banned in November 1980 and subsequently unbanned began with a phone call to my home in mid-October 1980 from Roger Tucker, who is the producer responsible for the Open University's 'Open Forum' programmes. In a 'distance learning' institution like the OU, in which the campus is the whole country, broadcasting can be used not only as an integral component of the academic courses but also to help give the students a corporate sense of belonging to a University. The Open

---

* Michael Pentz was trained as a physicist and electrical engineer. He has taught physics at Imperial College, London, worked on research for CERN (European Organisation for Nuclear Research) and has been Dean of the Open University's Science Faculty since 1969. Active in the peace movement since 1979, he is now chairman of Scientists Against Nuclear Arms and national vice-chairperson of CND.

Forum programmes, on extra-curricular subjects, serve this purpose.

Roger Tucker had a problem caused by the late withdrawal of Lord Asa Briggs (the OU's Chancellor) from an earlier commitment to give the third in the new series of Open Lectures. The venue and the outside broadcast unit were already booked for November 7, so, with apologies for the short notice, he asked would I help them out by taking Asa's place?

I agreed in principle, and asked Roger whether he had any particular topic in mind. He said he knew I had worked on the problem of energy in general and nuclear energy in particular, so what about that as a topic? I said that I had indeed done some work on the subject (though a few years previously), and at short notice I would prefer to lecture on a subject on which I had been doing a lot of work in the previous six months, namely the nuclear arms race. This was also a subject in which there was a great deal of general interest and on which, in my view, it was important that people should be well informed.

He agreed to this and asked me to propose a title, which I did, the following morning. I chose the same title as that of the booklet I had written earlier that year: 'Towards the final abyss? The state of the nuclear arms race'. He said that sounded fine, and we then discussed practicalities. At his request, I wrote out a three page outline to give him some idea of the ground I might try to cover. I told him that he should take this as merely indicative, not definitive, as I would not know whether I could cover all that ground in the time available until I had actually prepared, edited and timed the lecture. A day or two later I had a memo from John Greenall, the OU's Director of Information Services, who is also Chairman of the Open Forum Policy Group. He said: 'I was delighted to hear from Roger Tucker that you have agreed to give the next Open Lecture on television. Roger has told me that you have chosen to speak on nuclear arms under the title "Towards the final abyss?" To underline that this is not simply a political approach (although political points will inevitably be made), could I suggest that we sub-title it "A Scientist's view of the nuclear arms race"?'

I replied, a few days later, accepting this suggestion. In my reply to him (October 23) I wrote: 'You are right in thinking that the lecture will not have "simply a political approach", especially in the narrower, party political sense of the word. On the other hand, as you say, political points will be made − or at any rate points of fact about the nuclear arms race that have political implications, for it is hard to imagine a more "political" question than one which implicates human survival'.

Chriss Madden/Peace News

Nuclear disarmers cast their shadow, but not always in the media

I then went ahead with preparing my lecture and with helping Roger Tucker make the practical arrangements, particularly with finding a suitable person to preside over the lecture and with ensuring that there would be an adequate audience − including OU students and staff and some people who were reasonably well informed about the subject and could be expected to ask intelligent questions and make interesting comments. So, with Roger's agreement, I invited a number of London-based people (the venue was the Great Hall at Imperial College) whom I knew, colleagues from the OU, friends and members of my family.

Unsuitable for the BBC

The lecture was scheduled for 7.30pm on Friday November 7. Two days before, I had a phone call from Professor Godfrey Vesey, at that time Acting Vice-Chancellor of the OU, who told me that he had just heard from Robert Rowland (the Head of BBC-OUPC) that he, Rowland, had decided not to proceed with the recording of my lecture because he thought it would be 'inappropriate and unsuitable' for transmission as an Open Lecture.

Professor Vesey urged Rowland to reconsider his decision or, at least, to proceed with the recording so that the quality of the lecture and discussion could be properly judged, rather than being pre-judged, and then decide whether to transmit the programme as scheduled (on November 30). Professor Vesey told me that Rowland had refused categorically to do this, saying that he did not want to waste time and money recording a lecture that would not be transmitted. I told Professor Vesey that I regarded this intervention as outrageous and insulting, both to myself as a senior academic of the University and, by implication, to the University itself, since it suggested that I did not appreciate the difference between an academic lecture and a political speech. I told him I had only agreed to take on the lecture to help them out of a hole and that I had more than half a mind to tell them to stuff it up their jumpers (or words to that effect). Professor Vesey, who, apart from being a philosopher, is a very pleasant and courteous person, urged me not to do that, and said that he had already told Robert Rowland that he would ask the OU's own Audio-visual Department to sound record my lecture if I agreed to go ahead and give it without video recording. I agreed to this, but said I would first try to persuade Rowland that he was making a mistake and that he should accept Professor Vesey's suggestion, for to do otherwise would undoubtedly lead to a major row that would do nobody any good.

I succeeded eventually in getting Robert Rowland on the tele-phone at lunch time the following day (Thursday November 6) and had a lengthy argument with him. I told him that I regarded his action as an insult and that I was sure that the Open University's Senate would too, and if he wanted to avoid finding himself in the embarrassing position of having to make a public apology before the Senate, he would be well advised to take up Professor Vesey's not unreasonable suggestion. He said: 'You are threatening me', and I said: 'The situation is of your own making and the remedy is in your own hands'. For a long time he was adamant and would not budge — even when I pointed out that if the lecture was cancelled somebody from the BBC would have to stand outside the lecture hall door explaining to a couple of hundred people why this had happened, and that some of them might be quite cross about this and tell the newspapers. Eventually, he indicated that he would consider allowing the lecture to be video-recorded, provided that there was no commitment in advance to broadcast it as scheduled on

November 30, and we left it at that.

My own guess was that we would be going ahead with the lecture, so I sat down that evening and typed out a verbatim text. I would not normally give a lecture, whether televised or not, from a verbatim script, but from a series of headings. Under the circumstances, however, I felt that the loss of spontaneity would have to be accepted for the sake of making sure I did not accidentally say something that could be used as an excuse for not transmitting the lecture.

I heard from Roger Tucker next morning that he had been told to go ahead with the recording after all. So the lecture was duly delivered and video-recorded, as were the questions and a few comments from an audience of Open University and Imperial College staff and students plus a few score others, mostly from London. The recording was, I believe, viewed soon afterwards by the Open Forum Policy Group, and they were of the nearly unanimous view that the lecture should be transmitted as scheduled – the dissenting voice being that of the representative of BBC-OUPC.

Meanwhile, Rowland had written to Professor Vesey (November 7) to say he had, after all, agreed to the lecture being recorded 'so that the issue can be judged after the event'. In his letter there appears a point to which the BBC stuck subsequently with extraordinary obstinacy: 'You asked for my initial reason not to cover the Open Lecture. It is simply put. The lecture was neither referred to nor discussed with the BBC. The lecture was not formally approved within the OU's normal lines of communication.'

Professor Vesey was, understandably, not much impressed by this. In his reply to Robert Rowland (November 13) he wrote: 'Judging from what you said on the telephone, I thought that what led you to decide not to record the lecture was not so much "the way in which this lecture was arranged at the relatively last minute and the lack of discussion between the BBC and the OU about it", as the fact that it was to be a lecture by Mike Pentz on the nuclear arms race. I hardly think you would have decided not to record it if the last minute choice had been for a philosophical lecture by me on the concept of communication! I am grateful to you for changing your mind, and acceding to my request to record it. Thank you.'

In the following fortnight, I had a few brief discussions with Professor Vesey, but heard nothing from the BBC about their intentions. (Indeed, I never had any formal communication from the BBC at any point in the whole affair). By November 28 it was still quite unclear to me, and it seems also to Professor Vesey, whether the BBC would go ahead with transmission on the sche-

Frank

duled date, or at a later date, or not at all. The Open Lecture was in fact advertised in the current issue of *Radio Times* (in the usual small print) as being by 'Professor Michael Pentz', with the time, as originally scheduled, 10.10am on Sunday, November 30. The billings in the Sunday newspapers' TV columns remained unchanged as well.

Not surprisingly, therefore, quite a number of people tuned in their sets that morning, including several who had attended the lecture and taken part in the discussion. To their astonishment and annoyance, an entirely different lecture (a replay of one of the earlier ones) was transmitted – with no announcement, explanation or apology whatsoever. Ironically, as one of the many irate viewers who wrote to the BBC in the following days put it: 'The speaker who did appear seemed to be telling us that the public needed to be educated so that people can make an informed choice and so contribute to a democratic society'!

I was phoned by a large number of people during that day wanting to know what was going on. Since I had heard nothing at all from the BBC I was not able to enlighten them. I gathered that several of them had complained or intended to complain to the BBC, and I advised them to write to Don Grattan, Controller of Educational Broadcasting. That evening I was phoned by both *The Times* and *The Guardian*. Apparently both papers had been contacted by irate viewers who had the impression that the BBC was indulging (yet again) in some form of political censorship. As both papers were evidently going to publish some sort of report the next morning, I thought it best to inform them of the essential facts about what had happened, in so far as I knew them. I declined to speculate about the reasons for the BBC's behaviour, as I had not been informed by the BBC either of their decisions or their reasons.

The politics of education

The reports in *The Times* and *The Guardian* triggered a veritable avalanche of protest. I have in my files only a tiny fraction of the letters to the Director General, the Controller of Educational Broadcasting, the press and MPs, sent by all sorts of individuals and organisations. Even so, the file is a pretty thick one. Among the public political reactions, there were not only resolutions from various organisations (for instance, the National Executive Committee of the Association of University Teachers passed a motion on December 9 condemning the censorship of my lecture), but also some sharp reactions at Westminster. Neil Kinnock, then Labour's Shadow Education Spokesman, sent a letter to Ian Trethowan, Director General of the BBC, in which he said:

I was very disturbed by the press reports of the Corporation's decision to forbid the broadcasting of an Open University lecture by the Dean of Science of the University, Professor Michael Pentz, at the appointed time last Sunday.

It is clear that major issues relating to educational broadcasting have been raised by this decision and I must urge you and your colleagues in the corporation to reconsider that decision and permit Professor Pentz's lecture to be broadcast.

I have always felt that the Open University has sought to sustain the best traditions of freedom of thought and expression common to the Higher and Adult Education traditions of this country. As far as I know, the Broadcasting Corporation has actively supported that aim. The censorship which is explicit in the decision to cancel Professor Pentz's lecture is a most dangerous and reprehensible departure from that convention and it must devalue the University and undermine confidence in the judgement of the Corporation and its fitness to provide the medium for educational material.

I am not in a position to form a view on the content of Professor Pentz's lecture since I have not seen it. But it is worth noting that he is a distinguished academic who, whatever his personal convictions, has made it clear that he would not diminish his professional standing nor abuse the facility of a broadcast lecture by – in his words – 'indulging in polemics'. It appears from the Times report of these events (Dec 2) that a BBC spokesman offered the view that 'usually the Open University lectures were on education or related topics'. There could clearly be no justification on those grounds for refusing to transmit a professional lecture by an acknowledged scientific expert in an established series of special broadcast lectures unless the spokesman or those who briefed him has the most cramped and blindfolded view of what constitutes 'education or related topics'.

I understand that the Corporation is deliberating upon this matter. I appeal to those involved to take in full account the reputation of the Corporation and its special responsibilities in education, specifically with regard to the Open University, and proceed with the broadcasting of Professor Pentz's lecture.

This was followed a day or two later by an Early Day Motion in the House of Commons. 'This House strongly urges the Director General of the BBC to broadcast the lecture by Professor Michael Pentz on the nuclear arms race', it read. The motion was signed by six MPs on December 3, and by December 10 a further 18 had added their names. Meanwhile, MP Dennis Skinner had taken up with the Prime Minister a number of questions raised with him in a letter from Lt. Commander John F. Kennett, of Bramley, and the ensuing correspondence involved Margaret Thatcher (December 10), William Whitelaw (January 8), Dr. Rhodes Boyson (January 21) and David Barlow, The Secretary of the BBC (February 4).

The mounting pressure outside the University had its counterpart within it. An emergency motion was tabled at the meeting of the University Senate on December 11: 'Senate views with grave concern the action taken by the BBC in refusing to transmit the Open Lecture by Professor Mike Pentz, entitled "Towards the final abyss? A scientist's view of the nuclear arms race", which was recorded by Open Forum. Senate urges the BBC to reverse this decision and to transmit this lecture as soon as possible'.

The pressure on the BBC was obviously becoming intolerable, and by December 8 they had climbed down to the extent of agreeing to transmit the lecture at some later date, 'within Open Forum in a student discussion format devised in the normal way by the University and the BBC'. Alternatively, the BBC suggested 'if the University so wishes, the lecture can be seen in the context of an offer to the BBC for general programming, in which case the BBC would wish to follow the lecture by a discussion arranged along the lines of general BBC discussion programmes'. In the light of this development, the Senate amended the emergency motion to make the last sentence read: 'Senate notes with satisfaction that the BBC has now agreed to reverse this decision and to transmit this lecture as soon as possible'.

The BBC had meanwhile been distributing a multicopied 'Background Note' to people who had written in (including MPs) which they also wanted to be handed out at the meeting of the Senate. This document contained passages which were so misleading that, if it had been distributed to the Senate, it would have had to be accompanied by a document from the Acting Vice-Chancellor refuting it. Very responsibly, Professor Vesey took the view that this would only stir up more ill-feeling when a settlement of the whole unfortunate business was in sight, so he refused to allow it to be distributed. It nevertheless remained the standard 'hand-out' from the BBC. The key points in it were that the Open Lectures were seen by the BBC to be restricted to 'distinguished presentations about educational matters and particularly about higher and adult education', and that in the case of this particular lecture there had been 'a failure of communication' and the BBC had not been 'adequately consulted'. The clear implication was that the OU had somehow tried to 'pull a fast one'.

In a letter to Don Grattan (December 16), Professor Vesey commented on the differences in perception of the BBC and the Open Forum Policy Group (on which the BBC is represented):

On the more general issues concerning the Open Lectures, it does seem that there is a difference between the BBC perception of these, as in your note, and the perception of the Open Forum Policy Group, and I agree that we need to meet further to clarify policy on Open Lectures for the future. It has always been our intention that these lectures should be aimed at Open University students and staff, and they were not intended to compete with general service programmes, but there do seem to be two main areas of dispute: the scope of the lectures, and the way in which they should be decided on and set up.

On the first, it has never been the intention of the Open Forum Policy Group that these lectures should be limited to educational matters. Indeed, the Policy Group paper (OFPG/26/3), which went to the Policy Group over a year ago, defines these lectures as follows: 'It was felt that these lectures should be primarily aimed at the Open University community. Lecturers would be chosen on the basis of their being articulate and able to present a subject to a general audience. Topics might be general or specialist, but should be of interest to a wide audience and whilst ultimately lecturers should determine their own topics, this would be in consultation with the Producer'. I understand that the BBC has not expressed any concern about the scope of the lectures until the specific issue of the Pentz lecture arose.

On the second point, the way in which this particular lecture was decided on and set up was in no way fundamentally different from the previous Open Lectures or other Open Forum programmes. Hence I was rather concerned about your comments about inadequate consultation and a failure of communication surrounding the Pentz lecture. Clearly there was some failure of communication on this matter, but it seems to me that this was within the BBC rather than between the Open University and the BBC.

Meanwhile, the last efforts of the BBC to set up some sort of specially orchestrated 'discussion' in order to 'balance' the lecture had fizzled out in the face of practical difficulties. I had discussed this with John Greenall and suggested that he might gently point out to the BBC that if they insisted on trying to graft on an entirely new discussion, quite apart from the technical difficulties in television terms, how would they cope with the reactions of the people who were actually present and who asked sensible questions and made sensible comments, when they discovered that the BBC had edited them out. It would be a case of out of the frying pan into the fire, and surely the BBC's appetite for punishment had to have a limit somewhere? The matter was finally tied up by Professor Vesey in his letter to Don Grattan (December 15):

On the question of the particular lecture by Professor Pentz, I am very pleased that the BBC is prepared to broadcast this, either within Open Forum or as a general service programme. I have discussed this with John Greenall and Mike Pentz, and we all feel that the lecture should be broadcast as an 'Open Lecture' within Open Forum, as originally conceived, and should be followed by a discussion involving Open University students. We feel that the discussion which took place after the lecture itself is entirely suitable, and would help to promote a wider discussion among Open University students and staff which could perhaps take place in part in

Sesame and on Radio Open Forum. It would be very difficult and time-consuming to set up another discussion which was as good as the existing discussion, and I would be worried that we would end up with rather a flat discussion and a disjointed programme. Therefore unless you have very strong objections to using the present discussion, I would suggest that we transmit the lecture in full (there might need to be some tidying up of graphics etc.) and edited excerpts from the discussion.

The lecture was finally transmitted on Sunday February 8. The publicity was, of course, as low key as possible, with the Radio Times entry failing even to mention the title. But a lot more people saw it than would have done so had the BBC never attempted to ban it.

So much for the facts of this incident. What inferences may be made from the whole sequence of events? I am still not sure whether the BBC's extraordinary behaviour is to be understood in terms of a 'conspiracy theory' or a 'cock-up theory', although the latter does seem marginally more likely. In any case, I think this is a question of minor importance. What is much more significant is the spectacular underestimation by the BBC (at whatever level) of the realities of the political context. To choose this particular time, when a massive and extremely broad-based upsurge of concern about the arms race and the headlong rush towards the final abyss has lead to the largest peace movement ever in the history of Britain, when *The War Game* (banned by the BBC) was being shown to packed meetings all over the country, to choose this moment to ban an OU lecture on the nuclear arms race was, of course, simply idiotic.

More important still is the lesson that even the most entrenched positions can be breached by the pressure of public opinion. I have not the slightest doubt that the BBC was eventually forced to climb down because they were simply being buried under a massive protest. This particular battle was won by ordinary people who took the trouble to pick up their pens and write, by members of the academic community who stood up and fought for their principles, by MPs like Joan Lestor, Judith Hart, Neil Kinnock, Dennis Skinner and many others whose concern for freedom of speech and information is real, and by the hundreds of thousands who, though they took no direct part, had created the political climate in which this battle could be won.

School students, politics and the media

*Hilary James**

Schools Against the Bomb was born out of a course at King Alfred School, an 'independent' school in North London, known as the Politics course. A few years ago some of the pupils brought a motion to the Pupils' Council saying there was not enough politics in the school. As someone put it at the time: 'Kids in the sixth form will soon have the vote, but they won't really know what's going on.'

After a lot of discussions, and after collecting suggestions from various age groups, the course was set up by a small team of teachers. It is a non-exam course for fifteen to sixteen-year-olds (we run a separate course for the sixth form – also political), and we invite speakers, show films, discuss current crises and their causes and go on visits to factories and newspaper offices. We discuss, among other things, party politics, civil rights – especially the rights and responsibilities of young people at different ages, jobs, new technology, unemployment, unions, the police, the media, advertising, censorship, 'roles' of men and women, pressure groups, helpful organisations, third world problems, the energy crisis and alternative political systems. An important part of the course is inviting former students to the school to talk about their lives at work or at colleges and universities.

A lot of time is taken up with discussion of nuclear issues, the arms race and the arms trade, and each year we show Peter Watkins' film *The War Game*. As a result, in 1979 a group of students started to write to the BBC hoping to put pressure on the then Director General, Ian Trethowan, to show the film. This was the beginning of a campaign.

Why does *The War Game*, filmed in 1965, have such a tremendous impact on current students? Or on most of us, for that matter? There are other, more recent films which strikingly state the danger

---

* *Hilary James is head of history at King Alfred School, a mixed 'independent' school in Hampstead, North London. She has also been closely involved in the growth of Schools Against the Bomb.*

of nuclear catastrophe, like Jonathan Dimbleby's film *The Bomb*. But it is the images in *The War Game* which continue to haunt us, like the frantic parents pulling their children down under the furniture as the warning siren goes. One sixth former summed it up recently when she said, 'It stays in your mind'. Also, as Nicholas Humphrey pointed out in his brilliant Bronowski lecture, we can relate to a calamity on a 'man'-sized scale, whereas imaginary vast global catastrophe may leave us cold. *The War Game* shows a limited nuclear strike on *Kent*. If the film had been an imaginative reconstruction of the impact of nuclear attack on a much wider scale, we might not have been able to relate to it in the same way.

Moreover, the very fact that *The War Game* is most certainly out of date only increases its power. Groups of students sit still and silent at the end of the film as though glued to their chairs. Many say later, 'My God, if it was like that *then,* what are we facing *now*?'

King Alfred students were not the first to raise the subject of *The War Game* with the BBC. They soon found out that Duncan Rees, then organising secretary of CND, had taken up the issue in 1977. Rees wrote that CND's concern

... is not simply to present our case but to have the indisputable facts about nuclear weapons discussed. Governments the world over, including our own, have stated that a nuclear war would be an appallingly destructive catastrophe. 'The War Game' gives animation to those facts — in a way which actually understates the scale of the holocaust if anything.

It is surely at all times an act of simple human honesty and sincerity that issues pertinent to our daily lives should be discussed — even if these facts are unpleasant. Nuclear weapons are undeniably pertinent to our daily lives, as the 'defence policy' of this country is based on them.

Michael Swann, Chairman of the BBC, wrote back saying there was no question of the Corporation reviewing its original decision not to show the film.

Even so, the sixth form still wrote their long letter to the BBC urging it to show the film and giving their carefully considered reasons. The BBC replied (in February 1979) that 'the film was too horrifying for the medium of television,' and that 'it does not appear to us that the passage of time has produced new circumstances in which our judgement would be different were we to reopen the matter.'

However, by the Spring of 1980 the BBC seemed to be changing its tune. For in reply to another letter from the students it said that *The War Game* would not be shown because it was considered 'out of date'. By this time the tone of the BBC's letters had become acerbic and it advised the sixth formers to drop the matter. The students decided they would not lie down, and began to organise a petition.

Launching Schools Against the Bomb

In the summer of 1980 a group of students from King Alfred's held a conference with Frensham Heights School in Surrey (also private) to discuss *The War Game* campaign. It was decided to launch a movement for school students at a larger conference at King Alfred's in July. About a hundred people turned up, including students from about twenty different schools in London and outside. Speakers included Sally Davison, the new organiser of CND, Major-General Harbottle of the World Disarmament Campaign and Scarlett Maguire of the Campaign for Press Freedom. There was a showing of *The War Game*.

After this conference there were various meetings of students from London schools to discuss the future strategy and tactics of 'Schools against the Bomb', as it was now called. The students ran the campaign entirely themselves, electing their own officials and drawing up leaflets and circulars, and I usually only attended to give occasional advice. In 1980 they held a postal ballot for all SAB members to find out whether they wanted to merge with Youth CND or remain separate. They decided they wanted to keep their own identity.

The main aim of SAB is to spread information about nuclear issues among school students and young people generally. More specifically, all schools should have their own SAB group, get *The War Game* shown, attract sympathetic teachers to support them and invite speakers and theatre groups to school-based meetings. As part of this campaign, it also aims to attend meetings of local organisations – churches, unions, constituency parties, local councils, social and youth clubs – and to raise the issue of nuclear armaments. And by publicising its activities through street theatre, distributing pamphlets and by getting into the national and local media, it hopes to build up a network of sympathetic contacts and to put constant pressure on MPs and Councillors, and above all, on the BBC.

Eventually, in November 1981, SAB presented its petition to the BBC. This was planned months before but had to be postponed twice due to the 'blanket ban' on marches in the London area during March and May. There was a lot of bitterness about the way National Front marches brought down blanket censorship on demonstrations. The cancellation of two demonstrations was also costly, since SAB had to send circulars announcing the change of plan to schools all over Britain.

About 1,000 students went to Broadcasting House in Portland Place to present the petition, amid shouts of 'Tell the truth! Show *The War Game!*' They in included contingents from Edinburgh, Bristol, Ipswich and Newbury. There were about 18,000 signatures on the petition. SAB is still waiting for a response.

Several national papers reported the presentation of *The War Game* petition. SAB were pleased that *The Guardian,* for example, carried a back page story and picture of the demonstration. Yet this article, like so many press reports of peace marches, had a faintly frivolous tone, as though the newspaper was raising its eyebrows at the thought of 'punks on the march'. In much reporting of SAB activities it is hard to escape this note of condescension: 'What will our kids be up to next?'

However, Rick Rogers' *Sunday Times Magazine* article in the spring of 1981 presented students' views on nuclear issues seriously – and brought in a flood of enquiries to SAB. The article made the important point that those who were 15 when Rick Rogers interviewed them should be able to vote at the next general election, probably in 1984. It ended by quoting a student from Bolton, who said: 'At least we now have a generation of people who are growing up concerned.'

There has also been some serious factual reporting of SAB conferences and other activities by some local papers. The Hampstead and Highgate Express, for example, reported the launching of SAB in a sympathetic way in November 1980.

Censorship of Youth TV

Youth TV is a group of young people who want the young to play more part in the media – particularly TV. They claim that young people's interests are mainly ignored by television and that there are very few programmes which take them seriously.[1]

In 1980, Thames Television offered Youth TV the chance to present nine 5-minute programmes, and Sarah Kogan and Zadoc Nava, both sixth-formers at North London schools, were selected as presenters. The programmes ranged over a variety of subjects, from Amnesty International, and the beating up of two black school students in Soweto, to Islington Grapevine, a counselling service for young people, to Radio Lollipop, a station run by and for disabled young people. Two programmes dealt with young people's rights, and an invitation afterwards to ring in for a leaflet resulted in 20 phones being jammed for an hour and a half.

The last programme was due to be shown just before Christmas 1980. SAB were to be given three minutes to put their views – the idea being to look at the way young people organise a campaign. In the remaining two minutes Youth TV had hoped to invite young people to write in and say what they would like to see discussed on television.

The four sixth-formers chosen to represent SAB – three from King Alfred school and one from Hampstead school – had divided the time in this way: Sam Taylor commented on the dropping of the bomb on Hiroshima; Leda Franklin spoke about the proposed *War Game* petition; Ben Rogers spoke about SAB organisation; and Pete Best talked about his worries at the siting of Cruise missiles in Britain. Sam said ruefully to me later: 'We really put a lot of time and energy into that programme. Speaking for less than a minute doesn't sound much, but you think about what you are going to say for weeks'.

Two weeks after making the programme, the presenters were informed that it had been banned. Leda told me at the time that she had heard that Ian Martin, the Controller of Features at Thames, thought that the comments on Cruise were 'too contentious'. Zadoc and the other students were convinced that the programme was banned because of the comments on Cruise and the references to *The War Game*. Ian Martin said that the programme contravened the Television Act because it was biased. He claimed that the IBA's rules on impartiality would be broken by a one-sided examination of 'a divisive issue' like Cruise, and that a five minute programme was not long enough to cover such a controversial subject.

The absurdity of such reasoning is obvious. Thames made it very clear that it was studying a *particular* campaign and that SAB was a group working for disarmament. TV audiences would hardly expect opposing views in such a situation. (Those who like History might be reminded of Charles I's directive to his clergy that sermons should be on uncontroversial topics.) Zadoc was no doubt right when he said that the youth programmes were 'a token gift' from Thames.

It is interesting, though, that a one minute comment on Cruise missiles can so rattle TV. It is also highly ironic that, as *The Guardian* put it the next day, 'the programme would have carried an eloquent appeal for TV to put on *The War Game.*' *The Times* carried a short column under the heading 'TV programme on nuclear arms cancelled'. No personal view was expressed by the paper. *The Guardian* Diary, under the heading 'Thames washes out kids', had a longer column, sympathetic in tone to the students.

Zadoc himself wrote an article for *Socialist Challenge* in January, 1981 in which he expressed Youth TV's frustration over the censorship. He said that Thames offered Youth TV a replacement programme on caning in schools, but the presenters had refused this on principle.

What has SAB achieved?

Clearly SAB has so far failed in its original objective to get *The War Game* shown on television. On the other hand, it has achieved a great deal while fighting the campaign in increasing the political awareness of school students and in spreading accurate and up to date information about nuclear issues. The students feel that there are only two ways of coping with the increasing threat of nuclear war − you either switch off and pretend it's not there, or you get up and fight it. As a speaker from the women's peace camp at Greenham Common urged the young people in Hyde Park in November 1981: 'Don't let them shut you up! Just keep on at them!'

SAB now has members in about 300 schools in Britain, as well as supporters in the USA, Denmark and Belgium. Requests for information about the organisation come in all the time, and it has set up links with various peace groups, some of which are working towards the teaching of peace studies in schools.

There is a fundamental contradiction in our school system. We expect eighteen-year-olds to use their vote properly and to participate responsibly in society. Yet how are people to behave democratically without *experiencing* democracy as young children and as students, especially if they have never been taught about the way society works? It is significant that King Alfred School and Frensham Heights School, which together launched SAB, both have pupils councils, both have friendly and informal relationships with staff (in both schools the Heads, staff and students are on first name terms), and both have full discussions of important political issues and election of school officers by the students. In a large sense everything is 'political'.

Finally, it must be said that SAB *has* had a fair amount of publicity. There have been reports of its activities in the press and it has been given a certain amount of time on the air − on Capital Radio and on Radio One, for example. But where TV is concerned it has drawn a blank.[2] Surely the most vital issue now is more public understanding of the increasing nuclear threat to our whole civilisation? If the media had more courage and determination, and was truly as independent as it so constantly claims, then how vastly we could increase that understanding and perhaps avert catastrophe?

Corporate images: Dimbleby, the BBC and balance

*Crispin Aubrey/Edward Thompson**

The BBC has finally recognised the importance of the resurgent nuclear disarmament movement in Britain. In February, 1982, two substantial sections of the BBC1 Nationwide programme were entirely devoted to the organisation and politics of the Campaign for Nuclear Disarmament. This was the first time that the unilateralist movement had been given such considered coverage by the Corporation outside specific events or reference in films on general nuclear topics.

The films were not of a particularly high calibre.. They implied, for instance, that CND had 'emerged' at its 1981 march and rally in London − a clear misreading of the steady build-up over the previous two years. They also concentrated on the predictable bogey of Communist membership and influence, on splits in tactics and on the national personalities, with virtually no discussion of the actual policies of CND − unilateral disarmament, withdrawal from NATO etc. But they *did* represent an important breakthrough against a past record which has generally been poor.

Other contributors to this book have dealt with two specific examples of the BBC's censorship, or attempted censorship: the failure to screen *The War Game* and the controversy over Michael Pentz's Open University lecture. But how does the BBC's record stand up to a more general examination, and why has the Corporation's establishment so consistently failed to allow airtime to any expanded explanation of views opposed to present British nuclear defence policies?

One attempt to answer the first question has been made by supporters of END (European Nuclear Disarmament). In a circular letter to all BBC staff,[1] they listed a series of examples of what were

* *Edward Thompson is a historian, supporter of END and has written and campaigned extensively for a nuclear-free Europe. He is the author of 'Protest and Survive'.*

described as both 'sins of omission' and 'sins of commission'. The former included not only the well-known cases mentioned above but smaller failures to cover such 'news' as the 500,000-signature CND petition presented at Downing Street, the government's 'Spring Offensive' against CND or European ministerial discussions about the neutron bomb. The latter examples showed how contrastingly strong coverage had been given to overtly militaristic programmes such as *Colonel Culpepper's Flying Circus* (BBC2, Feb. 1981), a film about a group of ex-US pilots who re-enact such events as the bombing of Hiroshima, or the *Fighter Pilot* series about the RAF, in which nuclear weapons were described by a pilot as 'a bucket of instant sunshine'. Alongside these, the END letter set the rarity of such programmes as the 1981 Bronowski lecture by Dr. Nicholas Humphrey (which itself followed criticism of BBC policy) and a short talk on Radio 4's 'Woman's Hour' by writer Oliver Postgate. This last example – a short, emotional anti-war polemic – was not only repeated twice but reportedly resulted in more correspondence than virtually any previous item on the programme, a clear indication of public interest in the subject. (The END letter also received a public response in that almost 50 members of the BBC's film library subsequently declared their intention to organise an anti-nuclear group within the Corporation.)

But to concentrate on specific programmes, as END did, clearly does not tell the whole story. Most television viewers establish their attitude to world politics from the daily news bulletins, now a steady stream on all three channels. And their image of CND and the peace movement in general may well be more strongly influenced by the regular flow of news items than by occasional documentaries, invariably shown at off-peak viewing times, usually after 10.00pm at night.

It is therefore not irrelevant to contrast the treatment given to last year's national CND march – less than five minutes on BBC1's main evening news – and that given to, for instance, the collapse of Laker Airways – roughly half the evening's bulletin. Not only was the Laker 'catastrophe' handled with considerable sympathy for the people stranded, or whose jobs were threatened, but the background to the disaster was explained in terms of why it had happened. By contrast, virtually no explanation was given as to why 200,000 plus people might be assembling in the streets of London to register *their* anxiety at a potential catastrophe. Instead, a visual concentration was made on the bizarre and the disruptive. Nothing could have underlined more crudely the prejudice of the programme-makers against (even such large scale) extra-parliamentary political activity, especially when it challenges such a fundamental Western tenet as nuclear deterrence.

News coverage apart, that television *can* deal more sympathetically with the disarmament issue was shown by Yorkshire Television's *The Bomb*, a film conceived and presented by Jonathan Dimbleby and networked on ITV in November, 1980. This both came out strongly against current weapons policies and gave clear preference to the views of those who had worked inside, and subsequently rejected, the United States nuclear decision-making process. Its strength as a plea for disarmament has also been reflected in its regular showing at peace group meetings.

Meanwhile, one example not cited in the END circular letter gives a clearer idea of why the BBC's concept of balanced reporting has continued to tilt against disarmament views. This was the cancellation of an invitation to historian and disarmament campaigner Edward Thompson to give the 1981 Dimbleby Lecture on BBC1, a refusal which eventually led to the postponement of the entire programme.

Michael Heath/*The Sunday Times*

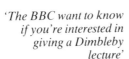

'The BBC want to know if you're interested in giving a Dimbleby lecture'

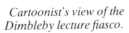

Cartoonist's view of the Dimbleby lecture fiasco.

Thompson was originally invited to give the annual lecture in June, 1981 — five months before it was due to be broadcast. In fact he was not the first choice as lecturer. After two other unsuccessful approaches this was to be Isaah Berlin, who then fell ill and in turn suggested Thompson. The latter therefore went to London to discuss the lecture with the programme's production team, and set to work on a synopsis. It was made clear to him that he should not talk about nuclear disarmament, since his views on that subject were well known, and he therefore chose the topic of the Cold War. By late July, having submitted his synopsis and received an affirmative response, Thompson was surprised to be told that his invitation had been withdrawn.

This outline of events, confirmed by Thompson, was at first strongly denied by BBC spokesmen, who claimed that no firm invitation was made and that a number of other speakers had been 'tentatively' sounded out simultaneously. In fact the Thompson invitation had even got to the point where a list of guests was being prepared and a request made for the full lecture text as soon as possible. The invitation had also been agreed, with no dissent, at a regular meeting of BBC executives, and it was only at a subsequent meeting of the board of governors that the then Director General, Ian Trethowan, announced his decision to veto the lecture.

Trethowan himself has never publically explained his justification for this veto, although it is clear that it did not meet with the approval of his deputy, Alasdair Milne. But three possible scenarios have been suggested, all political in origin. One is that the BBC faced an imminent, and crucial, government decision on its new licence fee, and therefore wanted nothing to rock the boat. Another is that there was direct pressure from the government to stop Thompson. Finally, it has been suggested that Trethowan himself was simply not prepared to let a 'unilateralist' give the prestigious lecture. Whichever is nearest the truth, the whole incident contained disturbing echoes of the *War Game* saga.

In practice, other evidence suggests that outside pressure on the BBC is unnecessary, since at least in the upper echelons of the Corporation there is reluctance to give CND-type views much airing anyway. After the 1981 demonstration, and the coincidental Brunowski Lecture, for instance, there was a lengthy discussion about CND at the weekly News and Current Affairs Meeting, attended by 30 or so senior executives and other staff from both TV and radio departments. During this, and having already noted that favourable comments about the lecture outnumbered the unfavourable by five to one, the Director of News and Current Affairs said that Nicholas Humphreys' talk 'had been an appeal for public opinion to express itself... (and) this pointed to the burden of the problem facing the BBC. More demonstrations would present further occasions for CND to seek to use the media to make their appeal'. In other words, CND was a pressure group trying to 'use' the media, and should not be treated at face value as an equal competitor for news space.

From the minutes of that meeting it is equally clear that not all BBC current affairs staff share this view. One in particular lamented the fact that Edward Thompson had not been allowed to give the Brunowski Lecture. So how does Thompson himself, who has experienced the hard end of media censorship, now view both his banning and the media's coverage of the peace movement in general? What follows is the transcript of an interview recorded in early February, 1982.

Crispin Aubrey: *How do you now view the whole Dimbleby lecture saga?*

Edward Thompson: Looking back, I don't think it was *that* important. But I do think it can be read in two ways. One is that the lecture wasn't broadcast, but the other is that there was a considerable attempt within the BBC to give me a chance to speak. So to say that the BBC as an organisation stopped the lecture is unfair. To say that there was an internal struggle in the BBC, during which the Director General over-ruled his own planning people, is correct. I think it's important that that is said. It wasn't the BBC as such, it was the Director General.

At one point during the argument a BBC spokesman also claimed that I had received a lot of exposure anyway, something like six or seven appearances. This turned out to be everything over the previous year, on both channels, even small mentions. But I *have* had coverage since, including a World in Action profile. This was done with real sincerity and a genuine attempt to be objective. That is why I resist a blanket condemnation of the BBC, or the media in general, because there's quite clearly a struggle going on inside.

CA: *Do you think that, partly because of the licence fee link, the BBC is closer to the establishment than ITV and therefore more subject to pressure?*

ET: Yes, I think it is more closely linked. But they're both absolutely appalling in their news programmes, with the BBC as the biggest outrage, and they're both extraordinarily Cold Warish in the way news is presented. This comes over in the domination of old Atlanticist types like Robin Day, who to my mind is one of the greatest threats to the survival of civilisation next to the missiles. Robin Day's whole tone and strategy of presentation is to imply a normal, consensual position which is pro-defence, pro-nuclear weapons, and anything outside that is considered extremist. This approach means that anything serious or objective about international issues — and I'm not talking only about something critical of the bomb — has to fight all the way to get heard at all, and then is subject to pressures to trim it in one way or another. Against that, the *normal* flow into both channels is based upon Cold War presuppositions.

As an example, you could compare the way in which the Reagan 'zero option' was presented, and the kind of people who were invited to comment on it, and the way in which quite an important speech by Brezhnev was rapidly glossed over. The only discussion I've seen of that speech was one in which a spokesman from the Strategic Studies Institute was brought in to knock down every single one of Brezhnev's proposals. Not that I think that Reagan's proposals were utterly disgraceful – I think they were mainly propagandist but still deserve some consideration – nor that Brezhnev's were utterly marvellous, but in fact the British public was not allowed to have any objective discussion of either. One was a good thing and one was bad.

It was the same with the Pope when he gave his New Year's Day message in St. Peter's Square about Solidarity. This was one of the main items on BBC and ITV news throughout that evening. But the Pope had also, on that same New Year's Day, issued a major statement of Vatican policy on the bomb, based upon the researches of the Catholic committee of scientists. This was scarcely reported in any visual or published media in this country apart from the *Catholic Herald* and *The Tablet*. On the BBC it wasn't mentioned at all and on ITV, after several minutes of the Pope on Solidarity, you had a sneering remark about the fact that East European and Polish television *didn't show* these pictures – all they did was show the Pope speaking against nuclear weapons. In fact, ITV was doing exactly the same as what it had accused the East Europeans of, and they *didn't* then go on and even tell us what the Pope had said about nuclear weapons.

So when I talk about the inbuilt bias of news, I mean that the information which reaches the British public is already polluted and corrupted at source. It goes through all these screens which stop us, for instance, hearing that the International Secretary of the Swedish Democratic Socialist Party recently visited Turkey and found that there was a minimum of 30,000 political prisoners, well documented torture, that trade unionists were coming on trial... This is a NATO ally and none of that, as far as I know, has appeared on the television news. The view of the world is wonky, and we have to struggle against this. In the particular area of nuclear weapons, because of the principled efforts by people inside, there has been some presentation of the issues, but in the face of immense difficulty.

CA: *On the 'zero option' example, no doubt the BBC's argument would be that they were presenting the negotiating stance of our American allies whilst what Brezhnev has to say does not come out of a democratic state, is stage-managed and not to be trusted. How do you counter those arguments?*

ET: This is really what *Beyond the Cold War*[2] is about. The basic ideological structuring of our major media, particularly television, is within exactly that set of assumptions, which is almost a religion. It's greater blasphemy to radically question NATO and the views of the Western Alliance than any religious blasphemy. And it's always referred to as if the only alternative to the Western Alliance must be pro-Soviet. A non-aligned position is a spook; it has no existence in the major media. It's sometimes denounced, but in fact it's never allowed presentation.

I know this personally because the opening essay in *Writing by Candlelight*[3] − which was about ideas of non-alignment in CND at that time − was rejected by the BBC Third Programme as a talk in 1960. I don't think much has changed in the intervening 20 years; but of course if I had been allowed to give that Dimbleby Lecture it would have been one of the first occasions that this simplistic alternative had been permitted by the BBC to be frontally questioned.

CA: *In 'An Alternative To Doomsday', an article you wrote for the* New Statesman[4], *you stressed how secrecy can prevent information coming out. How important is that as against a lack of investigative zeal among journalists?*

ET: I wouldn't write that article in exactly the same way now because there have been one or two changes. But what *had* happened was that as far as defence was concerned there was a total control of the flow of information − and that control represents one of the most significant forms of power. So that any enterprise in investigation was disallowed by the use of the Official Secrets Act, defence was considered the affair of defence correspondents, and those jobs were in almost every case in the hands of very compliant people who knew that they had nothing to worry about unless they stepped outside the official briefings. And if they *did* step beyond the bounds of what they were expected to say they wouldn't be invited to the briefings, so their information would dry up. You could check this by looking at *The Times*, the *Telegraph* and *The Guardian* in autumn 1979 and seeing that they've all got exactly the same official briefing, but afterwards perhaps may have done a little extra chatting up and added a little decoration to the story. But it was still the same story underneath. So we were being told what we ought to know.

I think there have been two changes over the past year and a half or so. Firstly, the cracks inside the defence establishment are becoming more obvious — inter-service rivalry, particularly the Navy versus the rest, but also genuine debate about whether we need an independent deterrent, whether Trident is going to gobble up all the money for the others — all these are going on and therefore you've got lobbies inside the defence establishment who are each trying to get correspondents on their side. This gives them much more room to play with, they don't have to tell the same story and they are actually *in demand* from those different interests.

Secondly, I think the fact that unauthorised investigations are going on — Duncan Campbell is the prime example — and the peace movement generally, has made defence correspondents realise that they are being watched very critically. David Fairhall in *The Guardian*, for instance, has been acting in a much more independent way and has made one or two very embarrassing leaks, like the story about the increased cost of the Chevaline modernisation. I also think that but for the peace movement he might not have got that sort of thing through; the Secrets Acts could have come down. And it's equally important to remember the victory in the ABC Official Secrets case, and the possibilities that has opened up for investigation.

CA: *There's certainly been greater coverage of the nuclear issue in the media generally, but has this actually reflected any change in approach?*

ET: What is the BBC motto, 'Nation shall speak peace unto nation'? That's important, because what does *not* happen is that the dissent in Europe is ever allowed to speak through these channels to dissent in this country. When you consider that at any time in the last six to nine months, opinion polls have shown well over half the Dutch people against all NATO weapons policies, on most policies half of the German people against, the Italians similarly, it's extraordinary that this kind of representative opinion never comes through. I heard a quite good programme on the radio about the German peace movement, but on television you don't generally get any presentation of this whole section of European opinion.

CA: *You've obviously been taken up by the media as a personality. Are you worried that you've been singled out, and the peace movement as a whole has tended to be ignored?*

ET: I'm immensely worried about this. One almost suspects some malice, some deliberate desire to trivialise it by personalising the process. On the other hand, it may simply be the way the media people work, that it's easier to structure a story round an individual. But when you see the way it's happened time and time again, how first of all an individual is elevated and then destroyed, you begin to wonder.

This is what happened with the Benn campaign last year, when every single issue of the left was identified personally with Tony Benn, and it destroyed his health at one point. And then with Ken Livingstone they tried to do the same thing. Just in terms of wear and tear, any individual on the left is simply not supported by civil servants, by a whole Office of Information, so it bears much more heavily than it does on some public person in the established world. So it either leads to a health crack-up or a mental one. I got to a point of exhaustion at the end of last year and I'm not through it yet.

And there *are* possibilities for conspiracy. For instance I was told that the Americans had begun to open intelligence files on prominent members of the European peace movement, which they now take very seriously. These are files in which they plant rumours – it's done very cleverly – and the sort of stories which are pushed out are those that are calculated to divide the movement, to create splits and jealousies. The story going round West Germany now, for example, is that I personally, and sometimes both END and CND, are financed by the Rockefeller Foundation and the Ford Foundation, and that we are an American trojan horse aimed at splitting the European peace movement. This could be a planted story or it could be a genuine rumour developed from the fact that we *did* raise some money in the United States for educational and informational work. But it shows how individuals can be singled out.

The personalisation of issues obviously does present difficulties which the movement has to try and sort out. It gives too much prominence to those people's own particular views, and this then leads to jealousy or dislike within the movement. It also leads to this ridiculous jam, this bottleneck, in which a few people are getting all the invitations to speak, they are the national figures, and the movement is failing to develop its next generation of speakers.

Louis MacKay/Merlin Press

Thompson's banned TV lecture was eventually published in pamphlet form by Merlin Press. It has sold more than 20,000 copies.

CA: *Do you think that the British government's anti-CND propaganda, and smear stories like the one from Dr. Joseph Luns that the Russians were pouring millions of dollars into the peace movement, have been at all effective?*

ET: I think that Luns' stories are ridiculous. There *has* probably been some Russian money into the World Peace Council in Europe, plus some rather comfortable junketings, delegations to the Soviet Union and Eastern Europe. But the real bribes, of course, exist on the other side. There are vast amounts of American and NATO money sloshing down the corridors of power, and the corridors of propaganda as well. This is where you're getting funding for the various phoney institutes. I think in comparison it's extraordinary that the European peace movement has been almost entirely self-financing – and independent.

On the question of Ministry of Defence and other publications *specifically* directed against CND, I'm interested in the constitutionality of this. I really think someone ought to refuse their taxes, perhaps I should do it myself, on the grounds that their money is being spent on specific propaganda by the state directed against specific voluntary organisations of tax-payers and citizens. I don't know how they can justify this. They are entitled, I dare say, to produce brochures explaining government policy, but are they entitled to actually direct propaganda against a voluntary organisation? That's where the money's being used – *our* money.

As far as effectiveness is concerned, the only government counter-attack on the peace movement which I know to have had any effect in the last six months was Lord Carrington's speech in which he said that the peace movement was weakening the position of the West in the negotiations about medium-range weapons. Because Lord Carrington tends to have a serious and practical image, and also has the reputation of acting in good faith over Zimbabwe, he carries far more credibility than any other member of the present government. I found some people in the peace movement genuinely puzzled and worried by this. Nothing else.

CA: *Do you have any advice for the peace movement about how it can handle the media more successfully and get its views across?*

ET: What I think is very interesting is the way in which we have put this movement together using the pre-modern media, and in the face of modern technology. By that I mean that we used the nineteenth century methods – the pamphlet (Protest and

Survive has sold well over 100,000 copies), the public meeting, the church hall gathering, the weekly press and so on. I've been to dozens of places where they say that they haven't had a meeting this big for ages. And this indicates to some degree a resistance to the modern media, a feeling that if you go out and actually see a speaker in the flesh you are once again participating in a democracy, a two-way process, whilst if you turn on the box this is something *they* are laying on for you.

CA: *What you're suggesting is that we might sometimes take the mass media too seriously, that it's not such an all-pervasive influence otherwise, for example, the peace movement wouldn't have grown as it has.*

ET: I think it *is* effective. It inhibits take-off. It makes it very difficult to present an alternative vision of reality, which is what the peace movement has offered. And to do that is not a thing which can be done every week, every year even. It has required a build-up of distrust over a number of years, a crisis of anxiety arising from the particular events of that time – and this has enabled take-off. But once take-off takes place, as it has, I'm not too frightened, because people get satisfactions, alternative networks of communication establish themselves and so on.

We have that now, and if you become influenced by the peace movement you have neighbours, you have a network, you have meetings, you have a whole set of contextual relations with people which can't just be turned on and off like the television. If you try and turn the peace movement off, the telephone rings or someone comes and knocks at the door. So that now take-off has taken place I don't think we need be too frightened about the media. I think we are influencing them back to some degree.

I'm not saying therefore that the pre-modern media are always going to be better. I don't think that we should surrender the major media at all. We should fight all the time for the right for these to be used as major channels of communication between the British people, just like the road system. But I think some kinds of information and argument will always travel on the minor road network – and get there.

Nukespeak: nuclear language, culture and propaganda

*Paul Chilton**

In totalitarian regimes, official state propaganda fills the hole of silence left by the censor. It is clearly and recognisably framed off from all other writing and talk. For that very reason it may not be heeded; people may even develop a healthy art of sceptical reading between the lines. Of course, propaganda in totalitarian states does not need to be effective: the army and the secret police are a more impressive short-term silencer.

In Western democracies, though you may be watched, you will probably not be imprisoned for expressing dissident views or un-palatable facts, and few people, I imagine, would question that this is a preferable state of affairs. However, contrary to conventional wisdom, this does not mean that in Western societies, censorship and propaganda do not operate, and operate effectively, despite the fact that there is no official censor or propaganda office. Noam Chomsky has pointed out that 'state censorship is not necessary, or even very effective, in comparison to the ideological controls exercised by systems that are more complex and more decentralised'.[1] Indeed ideological control may be more effective for not being recognisably framed off from the rest of discourse. To quote Chomsky further:

A totalitarian state simply enuciates official doctrine − clearly, explicitly. Internally, one can think what one likes, but one can only express opposition at one's peril. In a democratic system of propaganda no one is punished (in theory) for objecting to official dogma. In fact dissidence is encouraged. What this system attempts to do is to fix the limits of possible thought: supporters of official doctrine at one end, and the critics... at the other... No doubt a propaganda system is more effective when its doctrines are insinuated rather than asserted, when it sets the bounds for possible thought

* Paul Chilton teaches linguistics in the Department of French at Warwick University. He is planning a full-length book on the subject of nukespeak.

rather than simply imposing a clear and easily identifiable doctrine that one must parrot – or suffer the consequences.[2]

Chomsky is referring here to the way the American press excluded certain views on Vietnam in the 1970s, but parallels can be drawn with the manipulation of the nuclear debate in the British media, as the contributions to the present book demonstrate. Alongside simple exclusion, of course, there are the equally effective techniques of ridicule, de-emphasis, smear, and so on.

In addition to these methods of censorship, there is also the likelihood that 'the bounds for possible thought' about the nuclear issue are influenced in a more positive way – in the sense that both official and popular utterances about nuclear weapons and war use language in such a way that nuclear weapons and war are familiarised and made acceptable. This is the basic idea of 'nukespeak'.

To coin the term 'nukespeak' itself is to make three main claims. First, that there exists a specialised vocabulary for talking about nuclear weapons and war together with habitual metaphors, and even preferred grammatical constructions. Secondly, that this variety of English is not neutral and purely descriptive, but ideologically loaded in favour of the nuclear culture; and thirdly, that this *matters,* in so far as it possibly affects how people think about the subject, and probably determines to a large extent the sort of ideas they exchange about it.

Granted that nukespeak exists, one is led to ask who is responsible for it. Clearly not some Orwellian grammarian rewriting the English language in the Ministry of Truth. One way of answering the question is to see nukespeak as a symptom of the nuclear culture we have forged for ourselves, as an indication of the depth of its penetration into our mentality. The post-Hiroshima world has had to create new images and vocabulary to encapsulate the inconceivable – literally inconceivable – phenomenon of nuclear fission/fusion and its moral implications. The development of the atomic bomb was not a smooth transition from existing weaponry, but a catastrophic jump to a new order of experience in science, politics and everyday life. In 1945 it was popular to refer to this jump as a 'revolution' which would itself 'revolutionise' human behaviour, and to communicate about such matters on the fringe of experience and imagination places strain on our symbolic systems. The language used to talk about the new weapons of mass extermination was partly a reflection of an attempt to slot the new reality into the old paradigms of our culture. It was also no doubt a language that served the purpose of those who were concerned to perpetuate nuclear weapons development and deployment.

This is the second way of looking at nukespeak, to see it not just as a kind of mass response to a crisis of comprehension, but as a controlled response directed by the state in conjunction with other interested parties, and to see it as a means of constraining possible thought on the nuclear phenomenon. In the consolidation and dissemination of nukespeak the media are crucial, their function being to pass on nuclear language from producer to consumer along a one-way channel.

Once you begin to look closely at nuclear language, you get the strong impression that in spite of the scientific background, in spite of the technical theorising, most talk about nuclear war and weapons reflects irrational, not to say, superstitious, processes of thought. Myths, metaphors, paradoxes and contradictions abound. There is no time here to unravel all the complexities: I aim merely to point out some of the features and landmarks in the linguistic control of nuclear ideology.

The birth of the bomb

The first atomic explosion was at Alamogordo in the New Mexico desert on July 16, 1945. It appears that many of the scientists involved were genuinely overwhelmed by the spectacle and deeply disturbed by the implications. Many more people, scientists and non-scientists alike, were overwhelmed and disturbed when atomic explosions destroyed Hiroshima and Nagasaki later the same year. One soldier who saw the first test is reported to have said: 'The long-haired boys have lost control'. Others too have been impressed by the fact that the people behind the 'atomisation' (as it was sometimes popularly called in 1945) of Hiroshima and Nagasaki were civilised and cultured men.[3] Patriotic fervour, political naivety, and the myopia of scientific specialisation doubtless played a part.

But after the explosion, what sense did they and the general public make of the experience? Nicholas Humphrey has recently stated the question like this: 'I do not see how any human being whose intelligence and sensibilities have been shaped by traditional facts and values could possibly understand the nature of these unnatural, other-worldly weapons'.[4] One explanation – the one I want to outline here – is that it is precisely certain traditional patterns of thought which make it possible to come to terms with, if not strictly to 'understand', nuclear explosions. We have traditional ways of talking, myths, symbols, metaphors, which provide safe pigeon-holes for what is 'unnatural' or 'other-worldly'. This is a dangerous tendency in human culture, one which perhaps helps to explain the spell-bound ambivalence of our attitudes towards the bomb.

One of the physicists who left the atom bomb project when it no longer seemed necessary, Joseph Rotblatt, points to a related tendency:

While everybody agrees that a nuclear war would be an unmitigated catastrophe, the attitude towards it is becoming similar to that of potential natural disasters, earthquakes, tornadoes, and other Acts of God...[5]

Robert Oppenheimer, the director of the first tests, seems to have handled his own experience of the explosions in terms of traditional images. He called the first test site 'Trinity' – that most mysterious of theological concepts. (Interestingly, the sacred three-some has reappeared in the form of 'the Triad', that is the 'conventional', the nuclear 'strategic' and the nuclear 'theatre' forces of NATO.) It is said that he had been reading John Donne's sonnet 'Batter my heart, three personed God...' At the moment of detonation, so the story continues, a passage from sacred Hindu literature 'flashed' across his mind:

> If the radiance of a thousand suns
> were to burst into the sky,
> that would be like the
> splendour of the Mighty One...

And on beholding the monstrous mushroom cloud he recalled another line: 'I am become Death, the shatterer of worlds'.

This was not an idiosyncratic response. After Trinity an official report was rushed to President Truman, who was then meeting at Potsdam with Churchill and Stalin:

It (the explosion) lighted every peak, crevasse and ridge of the nearby mountain range with a clarity and beauty that cannot be described... It was the beauty the great poets dream about... Then came the strong, sustained, awesome roar which warned of doomsday and made us feel that we puny things were blasphemous to dare to tamper with the forces heretofore reserved to the Almighty.[6]

The religious vocabulary and phrasing are unmistakable, and are typical of the way the politicians and the press spoke later. In religious cultures the awful and the anomalous are allied with the supernatural, and the supernatural is both dangerous and sacred. Such familiar patterns of thought and talk somehow seem to have made the bomb both conceivable and acceptable. There is also another deep-seated cultural stereotype that has served to mythologise the sorry history of Oppenheimer himself, as well as to alleviate the guilt of the physicists. This is the stereotype of Faust, the overweening genius with dangerous access to the secrets of the universe.

Oppenheimer declared, Faust-like, in 1956: 'We did the Devil's work'. To what extent did he act out the role? He certainly appears, or is portrayed as, a late Renaissance stereotype – like Faust ambitious, individualistic, immersed in science and culture.

Some of the scientists may indeed have been mythologising themselves. Wiseman thinks that 'what they really were doing, and they must have been aware of it as they were doing it, was challenging the whole system of God and the whole of the Judaeo-Christian morality that up to then said certain things are prohibited by God'.[7] Others have cast them in the traditional roles. Lord Zuckerman speaks of the 'alchemists of our times, working in secret ways which cannot be divulged, casting spells...' In one recent film about Oppenheimer, his scientist-biographer explicitly describes him as a Faust-figure.[8] In traditional cultures such figures are dangerous; they have to be purged. It's therefore not surprising that in the McCarthyite witch-hunts Oppenheimer was ritualistically cast out of the body politic. My point is that the re-cycling of symbolic thought, talk and actions has helped to bring us to terms with the invention of the bomb. It is a dangerous game to play in the nuclear age.

It is important to realise that this re-cycling was fostered by politicians and the press. In August 1945 there emerged a new consensus language, speaking of the atomic bomb in terms of religious awe and evoking simultaneously the forces of life and death. One useful consequence of such language, if not one of its actual motivations, was to appear to diminish human control, responsibility and guilt. Its immediate political function was to obscure the fact that, strictly, the bomb project need never have been completed, and the bomb itself never dropped.

The problem, for the press, linguistically speaking, was what words to use to refer to the new thing, how to capture a new concept, but also how to conceal from the many the horror that had been glimpsed by the few. There is a kind of gruesome poetry in the resulting style. Rarely is the atomic bomb described in totally negative terms. When the *Times* called it 'the new and terrible weapon of annihilation',[9] this was exceptional. Some letter writers criticised it vigorously, but the contrary was evidently the editorial policy of the established papers.

Like the scientists, journalists expressed themselves in terms of incomprehension and ineffable awe. The *Times* called the scale of destruction 'stupendous', 'beyond belief', and declared its 'bewilderment'.[10] The verbal reactions of eye-witnesses of Hiroshima and Nagasaki were dutifully reported: ' "My God", burst out every member of the crew as the bomb struck'. 'The whole thing was tremendous and awe-inspiring' said a Captain Parsons of the U.S. Navy.[11] The *Daily Mail* spoke of the problem for the human mind in confronting what human minds had produced: 'The test for our survival... is whether the solution of the problems raised by the splitting of the atom lies within the human brain.' This was dismissed by the *Daily Worker* as 'mumbo jumbo', 'medieval superstiton' and 'mysticism'. Actually, both papers were making a valid point. At the end of the week the *Observer* gave a sermon on what it called 'a week of wonders', mystified the bomb by referring to it simply as 'A' (for 'atom', but also for alpha, source of creation), and compounded the mystification by calling it 'destruction's masterpiece'. Such paradoxical expressions abound in the press rhetoric of that week.

There emerged a small set of evocative, positively valued words for describing the bomb and its effects. They are interesting for the notion of nukespeak not only because they stretch existing meanings but also because their use often seems to originate in specific sources − politicians' speeches, and the public utterances of the military. The papers picked them up both in reporting and in comment, and not only repeated them incessantly, but spawned on them a whole network of associations and metaphors.

The press did not in fact, in the first instance, report Hiroshima and Nagasaki direct; it reported official utterances *about* them. The speeches of Truman and Churchill on August 6, 1945 were quoted verbatim, but they also provided the core of the subsequent bomb rhetoric developed in the papers. Two key passages in Truman's speech were seized upon:

It is an atomic bomb. It is the *harnessing of the basic power of the universe...*

and

The *force* from which *the sun* draws *its power* has been *loosed...*

The key words here seem to have triggered off a whole series of associations which have their basis in the language of religion and myth. Churchill, reported verbatim in *The Times* of August 7, provides an example of this, one that was to yield still more reverberations:

By God's mercy British and American science outpaced all German efforts... This *revelation of the secrets of nature,* long mercifully *withheld from man,* should arouse the most solemn reflections in the mind and conscience of every human being capable of comprehension. We must indeed *pray* that these awful *agencies* will indeed *be made to conduce to peace* among the nations, and instead of wreaking measureless havoc upon the entire globe they may become *a permanent fountain* of world *prosperity.*

So the select few capable of comprehending the problem are let off with 'solemn reflections' — that is, pious platitudes well illustrated in the surrounding verbiage, and copiously regurgitated by editorialists. How do the rhetorical tricks work?

Churchill does not refer directly to the event that inspired the speech, but instead to the 'revelation of the secrets of nature'. In the next few days it became commonplace to describe the development and dropping of the bomb in such a way as to make it a natural (or supernatural) process somehow outside human control. That perspective is underscored by a grammatical tactic — using the passive construction with no mention of the causative agent. The 'secrets of nature' have been 'long witheld'. By whom? When agents are omitted readers and hearers normally have to make an inference from context, if possible, and if not possible, make speculative guesses that are plausible in some framework of belief. Or, more conveniently, they can just leave the question unasked. Here readers are strongly encouraged (by words like 'pray' and 'revelation') to suppose that God was the agent. In fact, what Churchill left implicit was to be amplified for *Times* readers by the Dean of Salisbury in a letter on August 10: 'God made the atom and gave the scientists the skill to release its energy…' More 'solemn reflections' followed. A letter of August 13 actually amplifies Churchill's phrase 'God's mercy': 'By the same token it might be claimed that through divine grace English-speaking scientists were able to make their original discoveries of the vast source of energy…'

Thus one is left with the supposition that men were not ultimately responsible for the invention and use of the atomic bomb; it was given to them by some outside force. This is not all. In Churchill's phrase 'will be made to conduce to peace', there is no clear reference to who will do the making (God again?). Moreover, the atomic bombs ('these awful agencies') themselves, and not humans, are presented as the agents of peace or destruction. It is the bombs that 'conduce to peace' (whatever that means) or 'wreak havoc'. The final image ('perennial fountain') of life-giving water is a potent symbol in traditional culture, and is used to insinuate the belief that the bomb is a 'power' for good.

The *Times* leading article for August 8 gives some idea of how the catch-phrases and grammatical tricks could be used to construct a kind of poetic pseudo-solution to the problem. The mushroom cloud becomes a metaphor — and an excuse:

An impenetrable *cloud* of dust and smoke... still *veils* the undoubtedly stupendous destruction wrought by the first impact in war of the atomic bomb... A *mist* no less impenetrable is likely for a long time to *conceal* the full significance in human affairs of the *release* of the *vast and mysterious power locked* within the infinitesimal units of which the material structure of the universe is built up... All that can be said with certainty is that the world stands in the presence of a *revolution in earthly affairs* at least as big with potentialities of good and evil as when the *forces* of steam and electricity were *harnessed* for the first time... Science itself is neutral, like the *blind forces of nature* that it studies and aspires to control... *The fundamental power of the universe,* the power *manifested* in the *sunshine* that has been recognised from the remotest ages as the sustaining *force* of *earthly life,* is *entrusted* to earthly hands... the new *power* (must) be *consecrated* to peace not war...

It isn't difficult to spot the verbal and thematic similarities between this passage and the sources cited earlier. The methods are similar — the exploitation of familiar traditional images evoking supernatural activity, and the subtle manipulation of grammatical forms; and so is the general presentation of the atomic bomb as something paradoxically good and evil but predominantly good, and as something outside human responsibility.

One of the most prominent words in the speeches and press reports is 'power', closely followed by 'force'. Religious associations are never far beneath the surface. Here's a sample: *Basic Power of the Universe, the fundamental power of the universe, the new power, the irresistable power, vast and mysterious power, mighty power, power manifested in the sunshine, power for healing and industrial application, mighty force, new force, powerful and forceful influence...* All these phrases were elicited by the news of the destruction of Hiroshima and Nagasaki. The advantage of intoning the word 'power' lay in the fact that it implied both supernatural forces and at the same time beneficial technological applications. This way of talking, together with the failure to report the full horrific details (reports of Hiroshima and Nagasaki casualties were at first presented as Japanese propaganda), made it possible to conceive that the atomic bomb and its use had been a good thing. A *Sunday Times* book reviewer thought Nagasaki should be remembered as 'A-B day', but the ambivalence of current attitudes towards the bomb was such that he did not know whether it should be celebrated 'with universal rejoicing as heralding Man's entrance into a Kingdom of Power and Glory, or with a dirge'.[12]

The naming of the bomb

Describing the architects of the atomic bomb, Lord Zuckerman has said that 'the men in the nuclear laboratories on both sides have succeeded in creating a world with an irrational foundation.' This is usually taken to mean that the highly rational activities of scientists have led to the production of weapons with no clear rational purpose – weapons as technical solutions in search of a problem. It can mean too that the strategic doctrine based on, even generated by such weapons, is paradoxical or self-contradictory – MAD. And it can mean, as E.P. Thompson has written, that 'mystery envelops the operation of the technological "alchemists", "deterrence" has become normal... and within this normality, hideous cultural abnormalities have been nurtured and are growing to full girth'. The naming of weapons systems, seemingly trivial, well illustrates this last point.

The accumulation of nuclear weapons beyond the point strictly required in a theory of mutual destruction has been said to serve a symbolic purpose, in the sense of creating political and diplomatic advantage. But there may be more to it than this. I want to suggest that the publicly known nicknames given to weapons systems are a symptom of their progressive assimilation into our culture, and also that such names serve to advertise this fact to the domestic population. The way they do it is something like this. There are deeply ingrained patterns of symbolic thought (some researchers think they are innate tendencies of the human mind) which are used to organise, classify, and 'normalise' our experiences of the world. Such patterns are present in mythology, religion, and many other domains. 'When a human mind, even a scientist's mind, is overcome by bewilderment, it runs for shelter to the archetypes of pre-scientific thought...'[13] Thus while nuclear weapons represent the most advanced scientific thinking, their role in human affairs is handled in a sub-rational, mythological fashion.

The Cold War itself is deeply sub-rational, and the symbols used to express it reflect the fact. In a common image two tribes oppose one another – the Eagle and the Bear. To see how this is ideologically loaded, consider the contrasting attributes of these two totems: one soars to the skies, is wise, and all-seeing; the other is heavy, clumsy, stupid and half-blind. Weapon names are the mythological insignia of the two tribes, and there is a similar relationship between the two sets of names we have given them. Not quite all, but most of the NATO weapons are given two names: LGM-30F/G is also called Minuteman, for example. The nicknames come from Greco-Roman and Scandinavian mythology, and from the more recent 'mythology' of national history. They form a meaningful pattern. The nicknames given to Soviet weapons on the other hand are generally based on an initial letter and are designed to disparage or to be meaningless: Saddler, Sasin, Scarp, Sego Savage, Bison, Blinder, Bear...

As we saw earlier, atomic and nuclear weapons were perceived as awesome and incomprehensible. A slot in our classification of reality had to be found for them, and to christen them was the first step. Rites of naming are rites of incorporation into social life; the officially unnamed in many cultures, including Christian, are in a state of nature (as opposed to society) and sin; they are perceived as dangerous. But even before naming them, weapons are humanised. They have fathers (Edward Teller, 'father of the H-bomb'), though no mothers; they grow from infants ('baby nukes') to old age (NATO's allegedly 'ageing' forces) in a family ('the ICBM family'); they retire ('retiring Polaris force') and make way for the young ('new generation MX ICBMs').

The pattern of development of the names is itself revealing. There are four categories: human types and roles (less popular now); artefacts of human culture – tools, hand-weapons (increasingly popular); animals (never very much used); and gods and heroes (most prominent). The early atom-test scientists under Oppenheimer referred to the first atomic device as 'the gadget' – not strictly a name, but a synonym that made the momentous experiment feel familiar, homely and useful. And when the 'gadget' was accepted into the life of the nation in the form of a useable bomb, it acquired a name. The uranium bomb detonated over Hiroshima was called 'Little Boy', the plutonium bomb dropped on Nagasaki, 'Fat Man'. They were thus familiarised as amiable human stereotypes. But that was *before* the deed was done and the cataclysmic effects brought home. After the event there were new naming tendencies which reflected the sense of supernatural awe. The human designations lingered on, however, though their effect is now not only to familiarise but also to confer a military status and a patriotic role.

The 1960's saw 'Little Boy' promoted to 'Corporal', and later to 'Sergeant' (both of these were tactical, short-range missiles). At about the same time 'Honest John' also appeared in Europe, equipping BAOR and the French forces. Then there were the 'Minutemen', intercontinental ballistic missiles of which we have now had three 'generations', the latest having been 'MIRVed' with 200 kiloton warheads. The word Minuteman may not mean much to a European. To an American patriot it refers to the heroic militiamen of the American Revolutionary War who were trained to turn out at a minute's warning. Thus this inconceivably devastating weapon is given a place in national folklore. And if you didn't know about that, there is also the odd fact that the name of this particular missile also spells 'minute (small) man' – odd because that too scales down the weapon's size, and recalls 'Little Boy'.

Animal names are not much used. They seem to be largely reserved to designate Soviet weapon systems. But one is worth mentioning because it illustrates the often bizarre way in which nuclear planners elaborate their semi-coded talk. In the 1960's a system was investigated which could dodge ABMs (Anti-Ballistic Missiles). It was nick-named 'Antelope' – a beast that is agile at high altitudes. A further refinement was called 'Super-Antelope'. This had the notorious successor 'Chevaline', a name which ought to mean (in French) 'horse-like'. Its popularity may owe more to its stream-lined sound to the English ear, but it had to have a meaning too, and Lawrence Freedman notes that 'there is a belief in the Ministry of Defence that Chevaline refers to a species of antelope which is akin to a mountain goat and is supposed to share with the new warhead the ability to move in a variety of directions at high altitudes'.[14]

The symbolism of height as well as of depth, the symbolism of sky and earth, life and death, is contained in the structure of many traditional myths. But the system is plainer in the imposing *classical* names that accommodate our weapons of mass annihilation in the structures of traditional culture. There are the gods of the sky, thunder, blinding light, who are both creators and destroyers. 'Polaris' (submarine launched ballistic missile dating from 1950's) is the 'stella polaris', the pole star, traditional top of the celestial sphere. 'Skybolt' was a missile project cancelled in 1962. 'Thor' (an American IRBM kept in Turkey in the 1950's and early 1960's) was the Scandinavian god of thunder. 'Jupiter' (another IRBM, accompanying 'Thor') was the Latin sky-god of rain, storms and thunder. 'Atlas' (an American missile of the 1950's) was a Titan, condemned to stand in the west to stop the sky falling down – an uncannily apt expression of 'deterrence' dogma. The 'Titans' themselves (the largest of the American ICBMs, carrying a nine megaton warhead) were a 'monstrous and unconquerable race of giants with fearful countenances and the tails of dragons'.[15] Then there are the gods of the depths. The largest of the American submarine-launched ballistic missiles is called 'Poseidon', the Greek god of earthquakes and of the sea, who calls forth storms. Poseidon had a brother Pluto, the ruler of the Underworld, and the French have a mobile nuclear missile called 'Pluton', and a new 'generation' in gestation known as 'Super-Pluton'.

These names enable us to classify the 'unnatural, otherworldly' weapons, though the actual mythological classification still keeps them precisely in that category. But the more recent trend is to mythically classify them as a part of human culture rather than as part of nature (or supernature), which is alien, terrifying and dangerous. This is a return to the era of 'the gadget'. Nuclear weapons appear again with the names of human artefacts, though this time they are predominantly tools of combat with strong associations in national folklore.

'Trident' (the Mark II Tridents are high-precision MIRVed and MARVed systems which will arm Poseidon submarines) is not only the god Poseidon's weapon, but also Britannia's. The symbolism may not be without impact on some British minds. There is also a smaller, 'tactical' surface-to-surface 'Harpoon'. The highly significant technical innovation in the arms race represented by the cruise missile is called a 'Tomahawk' — though this one can travel 1,500 miles with a 200 kiloton warhead. From medieval military history we have the 'Mace', an early form of cruise missile developed in the 1960's. NATO forces in Europe are armed with 'Lances' — artillery missiles that can deliver conventional, nuclear or neutron shells up to 75 miles. And the neutron shell itself has been variously christened in ways that illustrate the present point. The term 'enhanced radiation weapon' is a rather unsubtle euphemism, and when Reagan's decision to deploy the thing in Europe was announced in 1981, the popular British press did its best to justify it. They did so in a way very similar to the naming process that produced lances, maces and the rest.

The *Sun* (August 10, 1981) said: 'It (the neutron weapon) will give Europe a *shield...*' Who would object to a purely defensive shield? We would, after all, not need a shield if there were no aggression. The *Daily Express'* Denis Lehane, in a piece entitled 'This Chilling but Vital Evil', shows how spurious arguments can be spun out from logically weak but emotionally powerful analogies. Lehane says he is seeking to rebut the charge that 'the neutron bomb is a moral evil... because it kills people but leaves buildings largely intact'. Here is his response:

Well, so does the *bow and arrow*! The neutron weapon is for Western Europe today what the English long bow was for Henry V and his army at Agincourt in 1415.

It is a weapon of chilling efficiency and destructive power which counter-balances the enemy's superiority in sophisticated armour...

There is a crude logic here which goes something like this. The neutron weapon destroys people not property. The long bow destroys people not property. Therefore the neutron weapon 'is' a long bow. But the long bow is good (and picturesque). Therefore the neutron weapon is good.

Comparison with accepted primitive weapons is not the only way in which nuclear weapons are classified as part of human culture, and thus as non-dangerous. The neutron 'gadget' has reportedly been referred to in some quarters as a 'cookie cutter'. Now to associate it with the kitchen and cooking is significant, because in our myths it is the cooked as opposed to the raw that marks human culture out from the untamed forces of nature. The natural and supernatural is also mythically associated with noise, culture with quiet, and 'Cruise' and 'Pershing', aside from their referential meaning, may well use sound symbolism to convey speed and civilised silence. 'Pershing', apart from being historically apt (he was the US commander who established the American Expeditionary Force in Europe against the initial opposition of the French and British in 1917) may well be onomatapoeic ('purr' in the first syllable) for some hearers. With these points in mind note finally that it has been said of the American nuclear superpower: 'You must speak *softly* when you carry a *big stick*'.[16]

There is then a trend in the 'naturalisation', or rather the *acculturation*, of the nuclear phenomenon. Instead of being symbolically classified as objects of supernatural awe, nuclear weapons now tend to be classified as safe and usable instruments. This shift has clearly accompanied the gradual shift in strategic doctrine towards a more pronounced doctrine of warfighting, of which the nicknames are the public propaganda face.

The bomb made safe

Like advertising, propaganda in western democracies has to sell a product. 'Deterrents', like detergents, also have to be sold. Taxpayers buy weapons in the sense that they choose the governments who buy them – though in terms of defence policies the choice has not been too broad. Of course, governments can spend your money without telling you (as in the Chevaline development and the Trident decision), but if the arms race is at all 'democratised', and facts about cruise, for instance, become known, then specific propaganda becomes necessary. When propaganda is not concealed in 'objective' and 'balanced' reporting in the media, it may take the guise of respectable advertising. One is reminded of cigarette advertising. Once people come to believe that cigarettes and missiles might be dangerous for them, the producers have to work hard to modify, eliminate or repress that belief.

When the plans to deploy cruise missiles became known during 1980, the population in and near the proposed bases received glossy brochures.[17] On the front is a drawing of a sleek windowless aircraft sailing through azure skies. It has no military markings. Unlike the familiar image of the missile pointed towards the heavens this one is horizontal, and has no tail of fire and smoke. Because of the way it is drawn, it appears to cruise silently past your left ear as you read the text. The first thing the pamphlet does, then, is not to explain the technical facts but to trigger a vague emotional response to the word 'cruise'. The dominant metaphor of the pamphlet is not, however, that of the travel agent, but rather the insurance broker. Beneath the drawing, in bold type, is the following statement: 'A vital part of the West's Life Insurance'. This odd metaphor is actually quite common in the parlance of nuclear strategists and those who advocate deterrence theory. Indeed, metaphors and analogies of all kinds are disturbingly prevalent in what is often claimed to be highly rational discourse.

It is not just that the association of 'Life' with weapons of death and destruction is bizarre. The expression 'life insurance' is odd to start with. You insure against theft or fire and you can insure against death too but you then have to call it not 'death insurance', but life insurance. The advantage of doing so is first that you suppress the taboo word, and second that you read the phrase (unconsciously no doubt) as 'that which insures, ensures or assures life'. Perhaps it is some such irrationality that makes the phrase effective in relation to missiles, since it scarcely makes sense as a literal analogy. If you buy an insurance policy, someone will benefit when you die; but it won't deter death from striking you, though you may have a superstitious feeling that it will. The supposedly rational argument that the cruise deterrent will ward off the death of the West is thus sustained by a doubly irrational metaphor.

The rest of the pamphlet follows the pattern of a commercial brochure. There is a series of questions and answers, or rather pseudo-questions and pseudo-answers, of which more below, and a wallet flap containing a separate leaflet, which does little more than repeat the material written on its glossy container. On the flap itself, however, is a colour photograph of a Transporter Erector Launcher (TEL) ('about the same weight and size as large commercial vehicles' according to the legend). Its raised pod forms one side of a triangle; a line of fir trees forms the other. The foreshortening reduces the impression of the length of the vehicle. A man in green

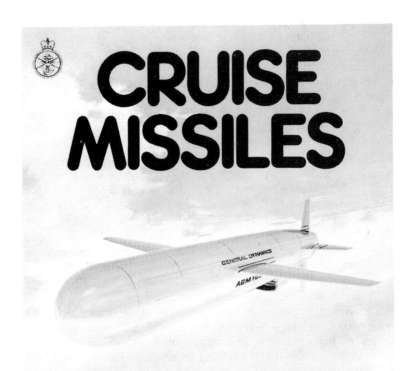

CRUISE MISSILES

A vital part of the West's Life Insurance.

We want to live at peace. The United Kingdom has for years sought disarmament through talks with the Soviet Union. But it takes two to make agreements and progress has been slow.

During this period the Russians and their Warsaw Pact allies have been rapidly building up their military strength. The Soviet Union spends about 12% of its national wealth each year on its armed forces. This is over twice the proportion spent by the NATO allies.

The Warsaw Pact countries have massive forces equipped with a wide range of weapons. They have large conventional forces operating with modern tanks, guns, ships and aircraft. They also have short and medium range nuclear weapons. Finally they have the very large long range nuclear weapons, which can be targeted from one continent to another.

We in the West must be strong enough to persuade the Russians that it would be too dangerous for them to start a war. But we have been falling behind. The weaker the Russians see we are the more they are likely to risk a war against us.

NATO therefore needs to strengthen its defences, particularly in medium range nuclear weapons where the Russians have now gained a significant advantage over the West.

By basing Cruise Missiles in the United Kingdom and other Western European countries we can go a long way to achieving this aim. Cruise Missiles are a deterrent. In an increasingly hazardous world the Cruise Missile is a vital part of the West's life insurance.

Front page of the Ministry of Defence brochure about cruise missiles: see
pages 107 and 110ff.

and dark glasses leans against the cab, and the line projected by his arms as well as the direction of his gaze intersects very low with the missile pod, to reduce the impression of height.

The back page is devoted to other aspects of making the weapon seem civilised and convenient. 'What will the Cruise Missiles do in peacetime?' We are assured that 'the exercises will be arranged to cause the least inconvenience to the public', and that 'busy road traffic periods will be avoided.' But 'Are Nuclear Weapons Safe? What happens if there is an accident?' You will be reassured to know that 'Nuclear Weapons are designed to the highest safety standards and (that) the greatest care is taken in their handling and storage'. The same might be claimed of television sets and electric light bulbs. However, in case any reader had some other notion of 'safe' in mind, he has the appropriate question asked for him: 'Will Basing of Cruise Missiles in this Country make us a Special Target if there is a War?' This and the preceding question are the only ones that expect a yes/no answer. The answer is 'No', and the reason is the 'sad truth... that no part of this country... will be safe from danger whether we have Cruise Missiles or not'. There is a good deal of fudging and hedging here, if not actual self-contradiction, and the fuzziness starts with the formulation of the question. Who is supposed to be asking the questions? Any British inhabitant, or specifically those near the bases at Molesworth and Greenham Common? Who is the 'Special Target'? 'Us' in Molesworth, or 'us... in this Country'? What the pamphlet seems to be doing is to deny that the bases are 'special' or 'priority' targets, and offering the cold comfort of a sort of randomised danger in time of war.

It is interesting that this, the most crucial question of the cruise controversy, is handled in this way. It is not just ignored, but raised at the end of the pamphlet, sandwiched between a 'question' on 'safety' and one on cost (in general, questions relating to wartime and peacetime matters are alternated and thus associated throughout the pamphlet). Moreover, the contradictions are scarcely veiled. But what carries weight in the act of reading is that emphatic 'No', which establishes an intention to deny and reassure: the reader will use that perceived intention to interpret the rest of the confusing text. This is a species of doublespeak, and its significance is clear in the light of the 1980 civil defence exercises, which included the cruise bases on their list of nuclear strikes.

The technique in the pamphlet as a whole is reminiscent of the distortions of 'balanced' reporting and discussion. Opposition as such is not silenced, but what constitutes opposition is pre-defined — the 'limits of possible thought' are fixed in advance, and the permitted degree of opposition is handled in such a way by those who control the medium that it is neutralised or marginalised. The cruise pamphlet sets up dissident questions on its own terms and knocks them down without possibility of reply. Most of the questions are phrased in such a way that they presuppose an assertion of the official view. The supposed questioner is made to say not 'Are nuclear weapons necessary?', which is the fundamental question, but 'Why are nuclear weapons necessary?' This presupposes the statement 'nuclear weapons are necessary', and places the 'questioner' in the role of tentative enquirer approaching someone with superior knowledge and authority. Similarly, (s)he does not say 'Does NATO need more nuclear weapons?', but has the question 'Why does NATO need more nuclear weapons?' put in their mouth.

No one will buy an insurance policy unless they are convinced that they are at risk. Hence the front page of the brochure is devoted to insinuating the Russian threat. This does not mean that there is no threat or risk − clearly there is − but the situation cannot be rationally appraised by dealing in half-truths and innuendo. the verbal techniques draw on the inherent (and necessary) vagueness of human language. When a hearer or reader interprets an utterance he assumes that the speaker has a specific intention and that he is speaking in relation to some shared context. This means that speakers can make indirect assertions, leaving readers to draw relevant inferences, while speakers can disclaim responsibility. There is the added bonus that insinuated propaganda is probably more effective than bald declarations.

Consider the principal actors in the front page text. On the one hand 'We'. In English this word is ambiguous: 'we' including 'you', and 'we' excluding 'you'. The actual situation is that 'we' (Ministry of Defence propaganda writers) are addressing 'you', but the reader is clearly intended to assume the 'we' includes her or him. Otherwise (s)he is committed to assuming that (s)he does not 'want to live at peace'. 'We' who 'want to live in peace' are then indirectly and directly identified with 'The United Kingdom', with 'We in the West' and with 'NATO'. Interestingly, there is no reference to the United States. The pronouns 'we' and 'us' are also defined in relation to 'they' and 'them', those outside the 'we' group. In 'we want to live at peace', the reader may be prompted by a number of contextual cues to stress the 'we', thus simultaneously inferring that '*they*' do *not* want peace. And the phrase 'But it takes two to make agreements and progress has been slow' infers that 'they' have been recalcitrant but 'we' have not.

Consider now the actions and mental states attributed to the principal actors in the various verb phrases. The vocabulary is not peculiar to the pamphlet, but is typical of the current rhetoric of the arms race. It is characterised by evocative vagueness, though a perusing reader may be left with the general impression of detailed definiteness.

Modal verbs expressing possibility, necessity, desire are most frequently attributed to 'us'. So 'we' '*want* to live', *seek* to disarm, '*must* be stronger', '*need* to strengthen' (implying that 'we' are not currently 'strong'). Cruise missiles '*can* go a long way to achieving this aim' — 'this aim' being a tortuous back-reference to the equally vague 'need to strengthen'. All this strongly suggests passivity, lack and inaction. 'We' also 'persuade' — a verbal activity; our military activities are limited to 'basing'; and 'we' 'have been falling behind'; in a modally ambiguous sentence, the Russians 'see we are weak'.

'They' on the other hand are not characterised by needs, wants and lacks, but by definite actions and possessions. 'They' 'have been rapidly building up their military strength'; the Soviet Union 'spends 12% of its national wealth each year on its armed forces'; and 'This is over twice the proportion spent by the NATO allies'. This sounds both authoritative and precise (all the more so because of the 'about'), but it is a misleading piece of non-information. Accurate information on Soviet military spending and valid methods of comparison are notoriously difficult to come by. The figures given are in any case relative — they take no account of the abosolute difference in 'national wealth'.[18] The main aim is not to inform but to induce the reader to infer aggressive Soviet intentions.

Note also the prevalence of the present and perfect tenses, which imply definiteness, reinforced by repetition: 'the Russians... have been rapidly building up... The Soviet Union spends... The Warsaw Pact countries have massive forces... They have large conventional forces... They also have... Finally they have... ' 'Their' weapons are described as 'massive', 'large', 'very large', 'modern', whereas existing NATO weapons are not mentioned at all. If 'they' is read with contrastive stress, as it might well be, the reader might infer from the statement '*They* also have short and medium range nuclear weapons' that 'we' do not have such weapons. However, the cunning pamphleteer has included an ambiguous 'also'; so that if challenged, he could always claim that he meant it to mean 'they as well as us'. Finally, notice the phrases 'to start a war' and to 'risk a war against us': it is 'they', the Russians again, who are the logical subjects of these actions.

The distribution of vocabulary and grammatical devices is systematic, but will probably go unnoticed. Most readers seem to store *meanings* in memory rather than words and phrases, and may not question the details. They will be left with the impression of a powerful alien threat to 'us', to their group. On these irrational premises is laid a spuriously rational logic. We are peaceful and weak. The Russians are warlike and strong. Conclusion: 'NATO *therefore* needs to strengthen its defences'. How? 'By basing Cruise Missiles etc.'

This is the first statement about these mysterious objects, or indeed the first mention of any NATO armaments. But we are not yet told what cruise missiles are or how they operate. We are told merely (for the second time) that 'the Cruise Missile is a vital part of the West's life insurance', whatever that can mean. More succinctly, we are then told that 'Cruise Missiles are (not 'would be' or 'might be', but *are*) a deterrent'.

The fact that they are classified as 'a deterrent', before their characteristics are divulged, is a significant ploy. It predisposes the reader to think of them in a certain fashion. In the first place, 'deterrent' seems to have become for many people in certain contexts a synonym – and a dangerous one – for 'nuclear missile'. So Cruise is classified first of all as just another nuclear missile – without the word 'nuclear' ever having to be used about 'our' weapons. (Equally the nuclear warhead and its explosive yield are never mentioned in the semi-technical details provided inside the brochure: the missiles just 'hit their targets'.) In the second place, in the single word 'deterrent' an important claim is made – namely, that the things do, as a matter of actual fact, 'deter'. That is to say, they prevent or hold back (depending on your individual use of the term) some enemy (the Russians, clearly) from doing something they are claimed, as a matter of fact, to be about to do – attack us. All that appears to be implied, in context, in the semantic structure of the term. Indeed, as this potent single word is habitually used, it encapsulates the whole cold war ideology.

The cruise missiles pamphlet is not an isolated example. Its rhetorical ploys are typical of current official discourse concerning defence matters and relations with the Soviet Union. Such discourse is scarcely conducive to a rational evaluation either of Soviet policy or of our own defence needs. Rather it is the typical stuff of which western propaganda is made. And it is all-pervasive. That is why much of this article has had to be written in inverted commas.

Media distortion:
how to change it

*Richard Keeble**

It would be absurd to attempt to separate the campaign against
media mishandling of the nuclear arms issue from the wider
campaigns for freer, more democratic and more responsible media.
The two are inextricably linked – just as the disarmament campaign
is so closely linked to wider campaigns for radical political, cultural,
economic and educational change.

Peace activists are correct when they accuse the mass media (bar
some notable exceptions) of distortion, censorship, trivialisation
and, more particularly, silence on the disarmament issue. But at the
same time ethnic minorities, feminists, socialists, trade unionists,
environmentalists and many other groups inhabiting the political
fringes, and away from the tame consensus centre, have equal
reason to complain. Thus the following analysis and suggested
programme of action relates specifically to disarmament – but it
can easily be applied to other areas of concern for radicals.

E.P. Thompson has described the recent mood of public debate
on the nuclear issue as a 'doomsday consensus'.[1] In his Bronowski
Memorial Lecture[2] of October 1981, Dr Nicholas Humphrey also
commented on the way in which the media were preparing people
for the holocaust. He described British society as being full of
'fascinated spectators of the slowly unfolding nuclear tragedy.' He
asked: 'Why, when faced with the nuclear threat do so many of us
adopt a policy of quietness and collaboration? Why do we choose
appeasement rather than protest?' Humphrey's answers concentrated on psychological factors – our sense of helplessness, incomprehension, fear of rebuke. But the points he made about the bomb

---

* *Richard Keeble is executive editor of* The Teacher, *a member of the JANE
(Journalists Against Nuclear Extermination) steering committee, an editorial
board member of* Sanity *and editor of* For Human Survival, *the newspaper of
the World Disarmament Campaign.*

could easily be applied to the mass media.

People have for far too long been 'fascinated spectators' watching passively the rise of the mass media to their position today where they are the most influential ideological formulators in society, the major source of information on the contemporary world. As a result, the control the public have over the media – as over the bomb – is minimal. This passivity has deep cultural and political roots.[3] But nowhere are the seeds more evidently sown than in the education system. Any programme seeking to transform media coverage of the nuclear arms issue has to be at first an educational one.

When will they ever learn?

Until recently the communications industry was subject to only sporadic, and superficial, critical scrutiny by both educationalists and political activists. Mass distribution newspapers and magazines, then radio and television were accepted by millions as the products of an increasingly sophisticated, technological society. They were passively consumed and enjoyed – and left in the control of the professionals and the wealthy few.

The education system, for its part, either ignored the mass media or regarded them with moral indignation. Lessons became 'innoculation sessions' against media evils.

Since the 1960s, however, interest in the media amongst educationalists has grown, if somewhat hesitantly. Pupils are increasingly being encouraged to approach media artefacts critically, to analyse the codings, conventions and mediation processes which shape media images.[4] Teachers throughout the service, from primary schools to universities and colleges and beyond to adult education, need to build on these advances. They need to develop media studies and to use media throughout the curriculum. But the teaching should not merely encourage a more sophisticated reading of newspaper and television images. It should have a dynamic dimension, leading students to question media messages, to demand better ones, and to create their own.[5]

Students themselves should not be afraid to break through the consensus of silence on the nuclear issue in schools, provoking classroom debate on the difficult and worrying questions relating to contemporary international tensions. Equally, teachers should heed the advice of the UNESCO conference on disarmament education in Paris in June 1980,[6] and place a high priority on adapting the curriculum to the needs of peace.

On the most basic level no pupil, for instance, should leave school without having learnt about the bombings of Hiroshima and Nagasaki. On a more sophisticated level, teachers should encourage co-operative games and a questioning approach to the sexist, militaristic stereotypes and attitudes which are still so prevalent in schools and text books.

Significantly, teachers' organisations, in particular the National Union of Teachers,[7] are taking up the issue of disarmament. The NUT has gone so far as to protest to the government over the scandal of education cutbacks at a time when millions of pounds are being spent on a nuclear arms programme, and to stress to its members the professional implications of disarmament education. Moreover, a Peace Education Network[8] has been set up to coordinate curriculum reform and to promote teaching and research in the field. A CND Teachers for Peace[9] group now has more than 700 members and is busy preparing classroom aids. A major peace education conference at Atlantic College, in South Wales, in 1981 devoted a special seminar to examining the way the media promote militaristic stereotypes and to suggesting strategies for teachers tackling this issue. These are all reasons for optimism.

From rhetoric to action

Peace activists have for too long indulged in high-flown rhetoric of contempt for the media. It is no longer enough. There has to be action at all levels — both against established media and towards the creation of new ones.

All peace groups should place a high priority on media work. In particular, activists should be well acquainted with the advice given by Denis MacShane, a former president of the National Union of Journalists, in his classic work *Using the Media*.[10] The writing of snappy, eye-catching press releases (complete with a comprehensive list of contact names and telephone numbers), the cultivation of sympathetic journalists over the telephone and through personal contacts, the correct preparation for and handling of interviews, awareness of media deadlines, the organisation of a news conference — all these need to be mastered.

Demonstrations have become the most popular form of peace movement protest. Originally worded banners, unusual costumes and imaginative demo props — the white cloaks, terrifying skeleton masks and cruise model carried by the women protesting at plans for siting cruise missiles at Greenham Common airforce base, was a particularly striking example — will certainly help win photographic coverage. Other imaginative activities, such as 'die-ins' to illustrate the horrors of nuclear war or in protest at seminars on nuclear strategy, are also contenders for coverage.

All the different facets of the local and national media should be exploited. 'Events' columns and 'What's on' radio spots should be used to advertise everything from jumble sales to public debates and demonstrations. And remember, events should always be described as 'open to all'.

At the same time it has to be stressed that peace groups should never fall into the trap of subordinating their activities to the trivia-obsessed demands of the media. Indeed, as the Greenham Common women found, the media are always likely to point two fingers up to peace. Reports of peace movement activities when they do appear rarely convey the complexity of the issues involved. For instance, much of the media interest in the massive CND demonstration in London on October 24, 1981 centred on its effect on the capital's traffic flow and the burden it placed on the police force, said to be more concerned to hunt out IRA bombs.

The media should be encouraged to examine the disarmament issue in as much detail as possible. A local paper, for instance, could carry a series of articles on such topics as: 'What would happen when a nuclear bomb falls on Blanktown?'; 'Could civil defence save Blanktown in the event of nuclear war?'; 'Doctors speak out on preparations for nuclear war'; 'Churches' views on nuclear weapons'; 'How teachers are coping with growing fears among children of nuclear catastrophe'. The list is endless.

And if the media seem incapable of producing the goods, peace activists should themselves supply articles (typed, one side of each piece of paper, with accompanying photographs, cartoons or other art work if possible) and tapes.

Peace breaks out on phone-in

Letters pages and phone-in programmes offer great opportunities for disarmers to spread their views. One remarkable success in this field was achieved by two women in Oxford.

For several weeks the women kept telephoning Dave Freeman, the presenter of a phone-in programme on Radio Oxford, about many different aspects of the nuclear arms race. After a while, Freeman came to recognise their intelligence, their deeply-felt commitment and their wide knowledge of the issue. As a result, the discussions gradually grew longer and provoked a great deal of public interest.

Recognising the public concern, Radio Oxford then went on to run a special two-part programme called 'The bomb on Oxford'. The first part presented the scientific facts about the likely effects of a megaton bomb on the city, together with the views of the pro-bomb lobby. The second part was entirely devoted to the arguments of the nuclear disarmers.

Wilfred Phillips comments: 'I was invited to participate in this programme, and at the briefing we were advised that the controller could continue for the full time allotted — one hour. If the interest was not apparent or the content good he could fade us. The hour seemed like minutes and the controller was delighted with both the content of the programme and the response from the listeners. This is just one example of the way in which, by using the phone-in programmes, we were able to secure air space for our viewpoints, with the added bonus of an hour-long programme of pure anti-bomb, pro-peace views being expressed'.[11]

Monitoring the media

Peace groups are obviously in the business of creating news. But priority should also be attached to monitoring the actual news.[12] There are obvious dangers. The operation can easily deteriorate into a pointless, time-consuming exercise, with countless cuttings and notes on radio and television programmes being filed away never to be seen again.

On the other hand, the exercise can be made both fascinating and educational, and the files can become vital campaigning tools. Perhaps a local peace group will want to establish how much coverage has been given to pro-disarmament events and speeches in comparison with pro-nuclear arguments over a certain period. An editor challenged over unfair coverage and presented with such detailed evidence will find it difficult to answer such criticisms. Careful monitoring will also help prepare groups to respond immediately to serious distortions and trivialisations.

Demand the right of reply

Denis MacShane, in *Using the Media*, lists a number of ways of effective complaining about media mishandling of an issue. He is right to warn people away from the Press Council. Since its formation in 1953 it has proved to be a toothless watchdog on media ethics, too closely bound up with the establishment to challenge even the most obvious forms of corruption that flow from Fleet Street's crass commercialism. The NUJ has withdrawn its support and it is best ignored.

A more hopeful move to help people misrepresented by the media has been launched by the Campaign for Press Freedom.[13] This is to give a legal right to any individual, organisation or company to require the editor of a newspaper which has carried a factually inaccurate or distorted report to print a reply within three days. The reply would be printed free and be equal to size and in the same position as the original article. If the editor refuses to print, the case would go to court to be settled within ten days. If the complaint is upheld, the newspaper radio or television company could be fined up to £40,000.

A Bill along these lines was introduced in the House of Commons by Labour MP Frank Allaun in June 1981, but was not debated. Allaun comments: 'This will not end the bias in most of the mass media, which will continue as long as ownership remains as it is. The Bill is no panacea. However, it will draw some of the claws of the worst press magnates. It is a limited but positive step'.[14]

Such a right of reply already exists in West Germany, France and Denmark. Peace campaigners should be pressing editors to reply in this way even in the absence of such a Bill — and in the meantime be putting their weight behind the CPF's vital campaign.

The Banbury Cake case: picket power

One successful campaign on media bias against the peace movement was pursued by Banbury CND.[15]

On May 21, 1981 a front page article in the *Banbury Cake,* headlined 'Nuclear hide-outs', reported on the launching of a nuclear shelter business. A certain Mr Tom King was said to be offering 'a choice of shelters all fully equipped to provide a comfortable standard of living for up to 20 days'.

The beginning and the end of the Banbury Cake *story.*

Most seriously, Mr King's virulent criticisms of CND went completely unanswered in the article.

By 10am the following day, 20 members of Banbury CND were outside the newspaper's offices forming an impressive picket, with placards and leaflets produced the night before. The journalist responsible for the original report also took a full statement from the pickets, which was duly carried under the headline 'Pickets hit back at shelter scheme'.

Another local paper, the *Banbury Guardian*, then picked up the story and carried a well-balanced double page spread on nuclear shelters and the rise of CND. For the next few weeks the debate continued in the letters columns of the *Banbury Guardian*. The local CND group's immediate response to the offending article, and its demonstration of the power of the picket, carries a number of lessons which the peace movement can ill afford to ignore.

Mediawatching **MEDIAWATCH**

In March 1981, a group called Mediawatch[16] was formed to help co-ordinate the media activities of CND and END supporters. With membership now spread throughout the country, the group is aiming to stimulate debate about and action against media distortion and censorship on the nuclear issue and to highlight good media practice by peace groups, such as at Oxford and Banbury.

A number of media workshops – for instance at the END national conference in Bradford in May 1981 and at the Nukespeak conference at the ICA in London in August 1981 – have been organised and drawn considerable interest. Some members of the group are concentrating on trying to pressurise the BBC into opening up the debate on the nuclear issue, highlighting examples of distortion and censorship, and inviting co-operation with peace groups to redress the situation.[17] The development of alternative media (videos, tapes, newspapers and advertisements) is also being encouraged by the group.

Alternative News

Virtually all peace groups now produce their own newsheets, though their quality varies enormously. The importance of establishing good, regular contact between peace activists cannot be over-emphasised. But the production of newsletters tends to fall into the hands of a chosen few. Ideally, the load should be spread as widely as possible, with workshops organised to help share skills and professional journalists invited to help.

More emphasis should be placed on making the movement's own press — *Peace News, Sanity,* the *End Bulletin* and *Undercurrents* — into lively, informative forums for debate. Following a decision at CND's 1981 national conference, strenuous efforts are being made to establish *Sanity,* CND's official magazine, as a viable monthly, sold through the major retailers. Such moves can only be welcomed, so urgent is the need for a rival to the appalling *Protect and Survive Monthly,* the glossy mouthpiece for the 'civil defence' lobby.

Advertising is a medium too often ignored by the peace movement, but the Peace Advertising Campaign (PO Box 24, Oxford OX1 3J2) is spearheading a highly imaginative campaign. One of its 10ft-tall billboard posters provides a bitter twist to the phrase 'nuclear family'. It shows a family pushing a supermarket trolley in which a few groceries are flattened by a massive Trident missile. The slogan on the woman's T-shirt parodies a famous slogan — 'Don't forget the H-bombs mum' — and the message continues: 'The average British family spent £16 a week on arms last year'.

Peace groups should consider raising money to buy advertising space in newspapers and they should press the broadcasting authorities to permit advertisements for peace. Not only can an imaginative advertisement press the case for disarmament in a direct way to thousands, but if membership application details are attached it can provide a superb recruitment aid and thereby possibly repay its costs. Handled properly, an advertisement, for instance including a long list of sponsors, could itself make news.

Films and video are other media the peace movement could be exploiting more.[18] Peter Watkins' banned BBC film *The War Game,*[19] and more recently Jonathan Dimbleby's *The Bomb,* have proved the dynamic potential of film as an educational and recruitment tool. The television technicians' union ACTT now has its own film company[20] and closer links should be established between it and the peace movement. The production of well-researched films for the fourth TV channel should also be seriously considered.

ACTT has in fact already provided a lead, which many other unions should follow, by establishing a special disarmament committee[21] to co-ordinate peace activities by the union. The committee has, for instance, organised the production of a film, *Together we can stop the bomb,* of the October 1981 CND demonstration and rally in London for use by peace groups and trade unions. A Labour Party fund has been established to produce a successor to *The War Game.*

CND publicity, national and local.

Unions for peace

The campaign for nuclear disarmament in the trade union and labour movement during 1981 culminated with the passing of unilateralist motions at the Labour Party and TUC annual conferences. Fourteen unions have affiliated nationally to CND – TASS, TGWU, FTATU, SOGAT, ACTT, CPSA, FBU, ASLEF, SLADE, NALGO, ASTMS, the Bakers, Sheet metal workers and Tobacco workers. Some specialist groups within other unions have also affiliated.

All this obviously represents only the start of the campaign. Many unions are still convinced that peace lies outside their aims and objectives. In these cases activists will have to argue for changes of rule. Massive efforts are still needed to win over the bulk of the rank and file to active participation in the peace movement.

Clearly trade unions should place a much higher priority on both peace and media issues, and media relations should be an integral part of all educational programmes for labour movement activists.

But a start could be made with their own newspapers, which should not only be viable, lively and accessible alternatives to the bingo-obsessed Fleet Street tabloids but significant forums for debate about nuclear arms. At the same time peace activists should strive to identify more closely with their trade union journals, inform them of their activities and utilise their letters columns and editorial pages to develop the disarmament debate.

Journalists against the bomb

One of the most important (if surprisingly little known) events of 1981 was the decision by the National Union of Journalists, representing the vast majority of professional journalists, to adopt a policy of unilateral nuclear disarmament. The annual delegates' meeting at Norwich in April agreed overwhelmingly to a motion[22] opposing cruise and Trident and agreeing to a national ballot on affiliation to the Campaign for Nuclear Disarmament. Significantly, the NUJ national banner was carried on the October 24 CND demo in London.

'   Much of the unilateral disarmament activity in the NUJ has been spearheaded by a group called JANE (Journalists Against Nuclear Extermination).[23] Formed at a meeting addressed by Lord Fenner Brockway, the veteran peace campaigner and longest serving member of the NUJ, and Duncan Campbell of the *New Statesman*, its membership now includes journalists in press and publicity work, magazines, local and national newspapers, radio and television.

Allegations in the journalists' trade paper, the *UK Press Gazette*, that JANE was a 'vipers' nest of Trotskyists, Marxist/Leninists and assorted anarchists' failed to prevent her from blossoming. Bruce Page, then editor of the *New Statesman*, told the inaugural conference of JANE, in June 1981: 'During the formative years of Britain's policy of nuclear deterrence any citizen in America reading a newspaper would have had a better knowledge of that policy than anyone in this country. This was a result of the deliberate suppression and manipulation of news by British official-dom, but it was also a result of the frivolity and professional incom-petence of the press. My hope is that groups like JANE may begin to change that situation and attempt to improve the sense of profes-sional responsibility among journalists'.

JANE's major activities have been in campaigning for support for NUJ affiliation to CND, challenging traditional views on profes-sional 'objectivity'[24] and 'neutrality', urging journalists not to par-ticipate in any work connected with the government's 'civil defence' plans,[25] and trying to open up the debate on the nuclear arms issue. A representative of its steering committee sits on the editorial boards of *Sanity* and the *END Bulletin*.

Clearly the activities of JANE are bound up with the wider trade union consciousness of NUJ members. This was graphically illustrated by Jake Ecclestone, deputy general secretary of the NUJ, at a JANE-organised fringe meeting at the Norwich ADM.

Ecclestone revealed that on one of his last days as a reporter for *The Times*, a news meeting had agreed that a JANE meeting, to be addressed by Melvyn Bragg amongst others, should be covered. But then the deputy editor had intervened, laying down that under no condition could a journalist be sent. Here then was a blatant case of media censorship, and yet *The Times* editorial staff had meekly submitted to the wishes of the depty editor. Until journalists have the industrial muscle and trade union consciousness to challenge actions like that, the struggle for a more democratic mass media will be frustrated.

Another practice employed by newspapers which should provoke protests from journalists committed to peace is the placing of in-house (fictional) by-lines over articles by persons whom, for some reason, editors wish to keep secret. David Leigh has exposed in his book *The Frontiers of Secrecy*[26] the extent to which MI6 and CIA-inspired Cold War propaganda is filtered into the mass media and from there into the public consciousness by these devices. Journalists should demand the right to know the origins of all articles over which in-house by-lines and pseudonyms are placed.

I also believe NUJ members have a responsibility to reject the use of what Paul Chilton (page 94) has described as 'nukespeak' – the bland metaphors, euphemisms, abbreviations and jargon acronyms used by nuclear strategists and their apologists. Phrases such as 'deterrence theory', 'civil defence', 'demonstration bomb', 'limited nuclear war' should never be used without the inverted commas. Television and radio journalists likewise should always precede nukespeak with the phrase 'the so-called'. These are just a couple of simple and obvious ways of suggesting that nukespeak concepts are not absolute truths but open to serious doubt, and of proving that journalists are not the gullible mouthpieces of the military establishment.

Militarisation indeed dominates, distorts and corrupts society down to the minutiae of the thought processes of individual men and women. Our minds are being prepared for the holocaust. We live in a society now ready to wage the war to end all wars, and nukespeak is the most horrendous of linguistic deformations because the horrors it tries to legitimise, prepare us for and dull our responses towards are the most horrible imaginable.

The military metaphor is probably the most prevalent one in our language. It saturates the mass media, and the media's preoccupation with violence, shock, sensationalism, newness has its counterpart in the violence of their language and the violence of the stereotypes (racist, sexist, militaristic) which they perpetuate. Just as enlightened journalists are now striving to combat the racism and sexism so appallingly prevalent in the media, I believe they should be taking professional action to combat the increasing militarisation of our language and culture.

Freedom of Information

One of the effects of the increasing militarisation of our political culture is that democracy has been dealt a grievous blow. Decisions involving millions of pounds, and effecting our very survival, are being taken by a few people behind closed doors. So no media issue is more relevant to peace activists than the campaign for a Freedom of Information Act.

Journalists' professional incompetence, laziness and misguided news values have all contributed to their appalling record over nuclear arms issues. But is has to be stressed that even for the many journalists determined to extract the facts, their job is made extremely difficult, if not impossible, by the hiding of defence-related matters behind closely guarded walls of secrecy. Legislation to break through these walls is desperately needed.

Secrecy has surrounded the nuclear power and weapons programmes since their very beginnings. The decision by an inner cabinet to proceed with the Polaris 'modernisation' programme, Chevaline, at a cost of £1,000 million during the Callaghan Labour administration was not officially revealed until early 1980 by their Tory successors. But the Chevaline case should be regarded not as an isolated event, rather as one that typifies the handling of the nuclear programme by governments and the military establishment, and the total contempt for democracy that this entails.

There is another significant aspect to the Chevaline case. On December 4, 1979, long before Mrs Thatcher revealed it in the House of Commons, Peter Hennessy of *The Times* was able to report the Chevaline cover-up. For alongside the appalling secrecy maintained by governments and the civil service over defence-related issues there has run the practice of 'leaking in the public interest' to certain establishment journalists. Governments are in fact engaged in massive exercises in news manipulation on the nuclear issue, with newspapers becoming urinals spattered on by the military's precious leaks. It is not surprising that the Defence Ministry employs more press relations officers than all the other ministries combined. As David Wood of *The Times* has written: 'The best Whitehall press officers, as one of them has been known to tell audiences at the Civil Service Staff College, are in the business to breach the Official Secrets Act and would be culpable if they did not.' (*The Times*, March 16, 1981)

The most appalling scandal of all is that this same Act, rushed through parliament at the height of a German spy scare in 1911 and repeatedly broken by the government and its Fleet Street lackeys in the lobbies, can be used to clobber left wing, peace campaigning journalists. Crispin Aubrey and Duncan Campbell were both prosecuted under Section 1 of the Act merely for having a private conversation with a former soldier, John Berry, even though nothing of the conversation was published.

Clearly the peace movement must place a high priority on campaigning for a repeal of the Official Secrets Act and for its replacement by a Freedom of Information Act, such as already exists in the United States and Sweden. The Act would place a statutory obligation on governments and public authorities to make information available to the public. As the Campaign for Press Freedom[27] comments: 'The object of a Freedom of Information Bill is not simply to help journalists in their investigations. Its fundamental premise is that in a developed democracy people need maximum access to the information available to government when it makes decisions in our name. A full access to the facts is the only way the public, including MPs and trade unions, can decide whether or not the government is taking the wisest decision.'

An ABC of nukespeak jargon

All Out Nuclear War	The end of civilisation.
Anti-Ballistic Missile	A bomb to stop a bomb from hitting its target.
Bent Spear	'Less serious' accident involving a nuclear weapon.
Broken Arrow	'Major' accident involving a nuclear weapon.
Cookie Cutter	The neutron bomb.
De-coupling	The Americans leave Europe to its own nuclear devices.
Defence	Preparation for attack.
Deployment	Siting of a nuclear weapon.
Deterrent	A nuclear weapon.
Double Key System	Two or more countries with their fingers on the nuclear button.
Dulled Sword	'Minor' accident involving a nuclear weapon.
Enhanced Radiation Warhead	The neutron bomb: kills people not structures.
First Strike Potential	The ability to hit them before they hit you.
First Use (of nuclear weapons)	A NATO 'first strike'.
Flexible Response	Political excuse for more, and varied, nuclear weapons.
Ground Launched Cruise Missile	One result of 'flexible response'. Also available in deadly sea and air launched varieties.
High Level Group	NATO inner sanctum of nuclear planners.
Independent Nuclear Deterrent	Expensive British (and French) collections of nuclear weapons of unclear purpose.
Intercontinental Ballistic Missiles (ICBMs)	Missiles capable of reaching Russia from America, or vice versa.
Limited Nuclear War	Much of Europe annihilated.
Linkage	American concept of political/economic response to Soviet aggression by e.g. refusing to negotiate on arms reduction.
Long Range Theatre Nuclear Forces	The ability to hit the Soviet Union from Europe, or vice versa.

Missile Experimental	The MX, latest American ICBM, no longer experimental.
Modernisation	New phase in arms race.
Moscow Criterion	The ability to hit the Moscow area, population 15 million plus.
Multilateral Force Concept	European cooperation on a 'credible' nuclear force.
Multiple Independently Targeted Re-entry Vehicle (MIRV)	Nuclear version of a shotgun: hits lots of targets at same time.
Mutual and Balanced Force Reduction Talks	An agreement to disagree.
Mutual Assured Destruction (MAD)	Both superpowers bomb each other to pieces.
New Generation (of nuclear missiles)	Another twist to the arms race.
Nuclear Non-proliferation Treaty	Failed attempt to stop more countries getting the bomb.
Obsolete Nuclear Posture	Argument for 'modernisation'.
Pacifist	Unprincipled fanatic.
Partial Test Ban Treaty	Tests conducted under instead of above ground.
Proportionality	Concept of lesser firepower of Europe compared to America.
Second Decision Centre	British right to fire its weapons independently of US.
Single Integrated Operation Plan	Joint British/US targeting of nuclear missiles.
Strategic Arms Limitation Talks (SALT)	US/Soviet attempt to slow down arms race.
Strategic Arms Reduction Talks (START)	New name for above.
Strategic Nuclear Guarantee	American 'guarantee' that NATO will be defended by its US-based missiles.
Strategic Sufficiency	Destruction of military targets as well as large areas of population.
Tactical Nuclear Weapons	Small battlefield weapons used on e.g. tanks.
Upward Evolutionary Adjustment	Yet another twist to the arms race.
100% Mortality Response	Everybody dead.

Beyond this book

This list of organisations and publications is a short addition to the many useful references in Richard Keeble's concluding chapter.

Campaign for Nuclear Disarmament,
    11 Goodwin Street, London N4 (01 263 4954).
    Publishes *Sanity, Campaign* (forthcoming activities) and numerous pamphlets. CND Shop, 227 Seven Sisters Road, London N4.

European Nuclear Disarmament,
    227 Seven Sisters Road, London N4.
    Publishes *END Bulletin.*

Armament and Disarmament Information Unit,
    Mantell Building, University of Sussex, Falmer, Brighton (0273 686758).
    Research group with cuttings and reference facilities. Publishes *ADIU Report.*

State Research,
    9 Poland Street, London W1 (01 734 5831).
    Research group investigating state policy, including military and police. Publishes *State Research Bulletin.*

Community Communications Group,
    c/o Jerry Booth, Hull College of Further Education, Inglemire Avenue, Hull.
    Campaigns for accountability in broadcasting and a 'third force' of low-cost radio.

Local Radio Workshop,
    12 Praed Mews, London W2

Women's Airwaves,
    c/o 125 Ashmore Road, London W9.
    Both offer help with making tapes for local radio.

Relay,
    Box 12, 2a St. Paul's Road, London N1.
    Alternative radio magazine.

Peace News,
    8 Elm Avenue, Nottingham. (0602 53587).
    Fortnightly magazine 'for non-violent revolution' with regular coverage of anti-nuclear action.

Get Yourself in the News — Using the Media in the Midlands:
    good example of guide to local media published by Birmingham branch, NUJ.
    Available from Charles Tremayne (NUJ Branch Sec.), 21 Coronation Road, Selly Oak, Birmingham.

Labour Party,
    150 Walworth Road, London SE17 (01 703 0833).
    Publishes series of useful pamphlets on the nuclear issue.

Notes

PEACE IN OUR TIMES?

1. For a fuller account of Edward Thompson's views, see page 82ff.
2. G. Donn, 'Report of a talk to Parents for Survival', December 1981.
3. As above.
4. L. Freedman, *Britain and Nuclear Weapons*, MacMillan, 1980.
5. From the press release of Margaret Thatcher's speech at the Town Hall, Birmingham, April 19, 1979, although Thatcher's statements of this sort have an even longer history: in that speech she made reference to 1976, 'when we warned the nation of the growing dangers of Soviet expansionism'.
6. Freedman, as above.
7. There are two useful books on this subject: S. Cohen, *Folk Devils and Moral Panics*, MacGibbon & Kee, 1972 and S. Hall, et. al., *Policing the Crisis*, MacMillan, 1978.
8. Jonathan Dimbleby's series of programmes, *The Eagle and the Bear*, could well qualify as one such attempt.
9. H.M. Enzensberger, 'Constituents of a Theory of the Media' in *Raids and Reconstructions*, Pluto Press, 1976.

THE DEFENCE CORRESPONDENT

1. 'Positive vetting' is a form of security check, including an investigation of personal and political attitudes, usually applied to civil servants working on defence or intelligence.
2. 'Ask yourself: would you press the button?' *The Observer*, Nov. 1, 1981.

CENSORED: THE WAR GAME STORY

1. 'The Conscience of the Programme Director', an address to the International Catholic Association for Radio and Television in Rome, Feb. 9, 1965.
2. As above.
3. Hugh Greene to Francis Noel-Baker, March 1, 1966.
4. Hugh Greene to Charles Mapp, Feb. 10, 1966.
5. Lord Normanbrook to a viewer, Jan. 13, 1966.
6. Hugh Greene to Allen Lane, March 7, 1966.
7. *The Ravenous Eye* by Milton Shulman, 1973, pp.242-3.
8. *Cine-Tracts*, Vol. 3 No. 1, Winter 1980, p.3.
9 .*Film Comment*, 1965, p.14.
10. Interview with Grace Wyndham Goldie, April 15, 1980.
11. Peter Watkins to Huw Wheldon through Stephen Hearst, Aug. 7, 1963.
12. Memorandum dated Jan. 22, 1965.
13. Head of Documentaries and Music Programmes, Television to Director of Television, Feb. 22, 1965.
14. Lord Normanbrook to Burke Trend, Sept. 7, 1965.
15. From a record of the meeting taken by Lord Normanbrook.
16. Robert Lusty to Lord Normanbrook, Sept. 28, 1965.
17. Oliver Whitely to Lord Normanbrook, Oct. 4, 1965.
18. Lord Normanbrook to Hugh Greene, Nov. 5, 1965.
19. BBC Board of Management minutes, Nov. 22, 1965.

20. From interview with author.
21. John Arkell said that the BOM decision had been referred to in *The Times* shortly afterwards. In fact, the only proximate item was a small article on Nov. 18 saying that the BBC would decide on the film in the next fortnight.
22. From a conversation with the author.
23. Sir John Masterman to Lord Normanbrook, Dec. 1965.

DISARMING THE DISARMERS

1. For more information on Mediawatch, see 'Media distortion: how to change it' by Richard Keeble.
2. For circulation figures, and details of control and ownership of the press, see *Using the Media* by Denis MacShane, Pluto Press, 1979.
3. See above and the TUC Media Working Group publication, 'A Cause for Concern', TUC Publications.

SCHOOL STUDENTS, POLITICS AND THE MEDIA

1. Youth TV has since presented a programme on divorce on BBC2 and been offered seven programmes for Channel 4. The group can be contacted via Hilary James, King Alfred School, North End Road, London NW11.
2. Since this was written, SAB *has* appeared on Open Door, the BBC2 access programme (Jan 30, 1982).

CORPORATE IMAGES: DIMBLEBY, THE BBC AND BALANCE

1. Further details of this initiative, launched in January, 1982, available from Graham Carey (West Yorkshire END), 6, Granville Terrace, Bingley, West Yorkshire.
2. *Beyond The Cold War*, Merlin Press, 1982, is the lecture Thompson *would* have given in book form.
3. *Writing by Candlelight*, Merlin Press, 1980, is a collection of Thompson's political essays.
4. New Statesman, Dec. 21, 1979, the opening contribution in *Britain and the Bomb*, New Statesman Report No. 3, 1981.

NUKESPEAK: NUCLEAR LANGUAGE, CULTURE AND PROPAGANDA

1. *Language and Responsibility*, Harvester Press, 1979, p. 20. Chomsky is specifically discussing Vietnam, but what he says applies equally to official doctrines on the cold war and nuclear weapons.
2. As above, pp. 38-9.
3. Cf. Thomas Wiseman, referred to in *The Guardian*, Nov. 5, 1981, p. 10.
4. The Bronowski Memorial Lecture. See *The Listener*, Dec. 29, 1981, p. 494.
5. Cited in *Overkill* by John Cox, Pelican, 1981, p. 10.
6. Quoted by Nicholas Humphrey, see *The Listener*, Dec. 29, 1981, p. 498.
7. Quoted in *The Guardian*, Nov. 5, 1981.
8. *After Trinity* by John Else.
9. Aug. 10, 1945, p. 5.
10. Aug. 8, 1945, p. 5; Aug. 9, p. 4; Aug. 13, p. 4.
11. *Daily Worker*, Aug. 8, 1945, p. 1, and other papers.
12. Aug. 12, 1945.

132   *Nukespeak: the media and the bomb*

13. *Robert Oppenheimer* by M. Rouze, Souvenir Press, 1962, p. 23.
14. *Britain and Nuclear Weapons,* MacMillan, 1980, p. 48.
15. *Dictionary of Greek and Roman Biography and Mythology* edited by W. Smith.
16. Denis Healey, reported in *The Guardian,* Nov. 6, 1981.
17. Available from the Ministry of Defence.
18. See *SIPRI Yearbook 1981,* pp. 147-169 ('World military expenditure and the current situation') for further comments on this kind of distortion, e.g.
    'One constantly finds, in Western discussions of Soviet military expenditure, that military spokesmen and others use the *dollar* estimate for the level of military expenditure, since that gives you a very high figure, and the *rouble* estimate for the rate of growth in that expenditure, since that method gives the higher figure for the rate of growth. This is, of course, not the only problem in producing sensible, and comparable, figures for rates of growth; one of the other main problems (is) the measurement of quality change...'
    Using constant price figures (rather than the misleading proportion of national wealth), SIPRI notes 'that there is a rough parity of resources devoted to military purposes...' It also points out that 'the one country in NATO Europe which had a military spending boom is the UK, with an average annual volume increase each year over the three years from 1977 to 1980 of 4.5%. This is an extraordinarily high figure...'

MEDIA DISTORTION: HOW TO CHANGE IT

1. 'Doomsday consensus' by E.P. Thompson, *New Statesman,* December 20, 1979, reproduced in *Writing by Candlelight,* Merlin Press.
2. The Bronowski Memorial Lecture: 'Four minutes to midnight', *The Listener,* October 29, 1981. See also 'Heretics on the box' by Albert Hunt, *New Society,* November 5, 1981.
3. Peter Watkins on the banning of his film *The War Game* in *The Guardian,* December 6, 1980.
4. 'Real entertainment: the Iranian Embassy siege' by C. Bazalgette and R. Paterson, *Screen Education* No. 37, 1981.
5. *Viewpoint 2 Pupil Guide* by A. Bethel, Thames Television; *Teaching about Television* by Len Masterman, Macmillan; *Power Without Responsibility* by J. Curran and J. Seaton (one of the best histories of the rise of the press empires and broadcasting institutions); *Bad News* and *More Bad News* by the Glasgow Media Group, Routledge and Kegan Paul; *On Television* by Stuart Hood, Pluto Press; *Mass Media and the Secondary School* by G. Murdock and G. Phelps, Macmillan.
6. *Approaching Disarmament Education,* edited by Magnus Haavelsrud, Westbury House.
7. *Education for Peace: a Discussion Document,* National Union of Teachers.
8. Peace Education Network: membership secretary, Dr David Hicks, St Martins College, Lancaster LA1 3JD.
9. Teachers for Peace: c/o CND, 11 Goodwin Street, London N4.
10. *Using the Media* by Denis MacShane, Pluto Press.
11. Mediawatch bulletin for July 8, 1981, Mediawatch, 6 Endsleigh Street, London WC1.
12. A number of cuttings facilities are open to peace campaigners. One of these is operated by North Staffordshire CND. Details from Alan Leadbetter, 8 Madison Street, Tunstall, Stoke on Trent.
13. *The Right of Reply,* Campaign for Press Freedom, 274/288 London Road, Hadleigh, Essex, SS7 2DE.
14. *Free Press,* bulletin of the Campaign for Press Freedom, July/August 1981.

15. 'Banbury CND unmasks fallout shelter con', Mediawatch case study No. 1, see above.
16. Report of inaugural conference of Mediawatch, March 21, 1981, see above.
17. 'The Nuclear disarmament movement and the process of changing television' by B. Davey, in Mediawatch bulletin for July 8, 1981.
18. Concorde Films have a large number of films on peace related issues for hire from: Concorde Film Council, 201 Felixstowe Road, Ipswich, Suffolk.
19. *What do we do after we've shown the War Game: a disarmament action manual* compiled by Daniel Plesch, CND, 11 Goodwin Street, London N4.
20. ACT Films, 2 Soho Square, London W1V 6DD.
21. ACTT disarmament committee, c/o ACTT, 2 Soho Square, London W1.
22. Full text of the motion agreed by the annual conference of the NUJ: 'This ADM believes that the NUJ, through the TUC and CND, should oppose the siting of cruise missiles in Britain and Ireland and the purchase of Trident missiles. This ADM instructs the NEC to do all in its power to campaign against the arms race. It notes the threat to NUJ members posed by nuclear weapons and calls for unilateral disarmament by Britain, and agrees to hold a referendum of the union's members with a view to affiliating to the Campaign for Unilateral Nuclear Disarmament.
    Accordingly ADM instructs the general secretary to write to:
    a) the Prime Minister expressing our total opposition to nuclear weapons in Britain and
    b) Mr Michael Foot, expressing our full support for any measures designed to rid this country of nuclear weapons and
    c) the Presidents of the USA, USSR and France and the Prime Minister of China expressing our total opposition to nuclear weapons in their countries.'
23. JANE, c/o Magazine branch, National Union of Journalists, Acorn House, 314 Grays Inn Road, London WC1.
24. A devastating critique of the 'objectivity' myth is provided by Brian Whitaker in *News Ltd,* Minority Press Group Series No. 5.
25. The government's pamphlet *Civil Defence — Why We Need It* says: 'A wartime broadcast service would be brought into operation to transmit public information virtually non-stop. The advice would be — Tune in and listen. Newspapers, television and radio would carry detailed advice on how to protect yourself and your family within your own home.'
26. *The Frontiers of Secrecy* by David Leigh, Junction Books.
27. *Towards Press Freedom,* Campaign for Press Freedom, see above.

Comedia Publishing Group
9 Poland St, London W1

Comedia Publishing produces books on all aspects of the media including: the press and publishing; TV, radio and film; and the impact of new communications technology.
The Comedia publishing series is based on contemporary research of relevance to media and communications studies courses, though it is also aimed at general readers, activists and specialists in the field.
The series is exceptional because it spans the media from the mainstream and commercial to the oppositional, radical and ephemeral.

New titles

No. 9.   Nukespeak – The media and the bomb
Edited by Crispin Aubrey
paperback £2.50 hardback £7.50

No. 8.   NOT the BBC/IBA – The case for community radio
by Simon Partridge
The rise of the community politics and media movements has rekindled interest in a new form of local radio.
The book describes the existing BBC and IBA structures and makes the case for a much more local democratic and accountable system, where there is far more scope for audience involvement. It describes how the idea came about and examples of how it can work both at home and abroad.
Part 2 is a comprehensive guide of how to put the idea into practice.
paperback £1.95 hardback £5.00

No. 7.   PRINT – An industry in crisis
by Frank Elston, Alan Marshall
Chronicles the history of the developments in print technology and how it has affected the relations between both workers and management.
Explores through case studies the current crisis in the industry and how recent changes are likely to shape the print industry's future.
paperback £2.25 hardback £7.50

No. 6.   THE REPUBLIC OF LETTERS – Working class writing and local publishing
edited by Dave Morley and Ken Worpole
Examines how in recent years, working class people, particularly women and black people, have begun to develop new forms of writing, new modes of local, collective publishing, alternative distribution networks – the elements of a movement which aims to

'disestablish' literature, making writing a popular form of expression, not the preserve of a privileged metropolitan elite. Many of the people involved in these projects have, since 1976, been working together in the Federation of Worker Writers and Community Publishers.

paperback £2.95 hardback £8.50

Also available

No. 5. **NEWS LTD. – Why you can't read all about it**
by Brian Whitaker
paperback £3.25 hardback £9.50

No. 4. **ROLLING OUR OWN – Women as printers, publishers and distributors**
by Eileen Cadman, Gail Chester, Agnes Pivot
paperback £2.25 hardback £7.50

No. 3. **THE OTHER SECRET SERVICE – Press distribution and press censorship**
by Liz Cooper, Charles Landry, Dave Berry
paperback only £0.80

No. 2. **WHERE IS THE OTHER NEWS – The news trade and the radical press**
by Dave Berry, Liz Cooper, Charles Landry
paperback £1.75 hardback £4.50

No. 1. **HERE IS THE OTHER NEWS – Challenges to the local commercial press**
by Crispin Aubrey, Charles Landry, Dave Morley
paperback £1.75 hardback £3.50